MILNER CRAFT SERIES

Decorative Embroidery

FOR GARMENTS AND HEIRLOOMS

DIANE BALDWIN

SALLY MILNER PUBLISHING

First published in 1991 by
Sally Milner Publishing Pty Ltd
17 Wharf Road
Birchgrove NSW 2041 Australia

Reprinted 1992

© Diane Baldwin, 1991

Production by Sylvana Scannapiego,
Island Graphics
Design by Gatya Kelly, Doric Order
Illustrations by Kate Edwards
Photography by Malcolm Cross & Associates
Typeset in Australia by Asset Typesetting Pty Ltd
Printed in Australia by Impact Printing

National Library of Australia
Cataloguing-in-Publication data:

Baldwin, Diane,
    Decorative embroidery for garments and heirlooms.

ISBN 1 86351 046 X.

1. Embroidery — Patterns. I. Title.

746.44041

All rights reserved. No part of this publication may be reproduced, stored in a retrieval system or transmitted in any form or by any means, electronic, mechanical, photocopying, recording or otherwise, without prior written permission of the copyright holders.

CONTENTS

Introduction   1
Accessories for Excellence   3
Fabrics and Threads   6
Transfer Methods   8
Stitches   11
Design Considerations   22
Helpful Hints   23

Projects and Designs
— Baby's navy knit jumper and leggings   26
— Detachable yoke for baby's garment   28
— Baby's cotton blanket   30
— Dressing table set, brooch and gloves   32
— Grandma's house – trinket pot   36
— White cardigan   38
— Navy knit cardigan   42
— Soft-pink knit jumper   46
— Cream knit jumper   50
— Navy cotton-knit jumper   54
— Black fine-knit jumper   56

Thread Grid   59

DEDICATION

First, I would like to thank a very special member of my family for his encouragement of my pursuit of excellence in the area of needlework. This person is my father, who so sadly passed away without knowing of my inspiration to produce this book.

I would also like to thank my mother for her continued reassurance of my creative ability, and my husband, Noel, for his support and patience during the compilation of this title.

Also, to Sarah-Jane, our daughter, who was born while the book was only partially written — I hope it will be an inspiration for her in the future.

INTRODUCTION

This book is an exercise in creativity. It is based on my own experience of developing embroidery as a decorative form. I have included what I feel is necessary to help beginners and embroiderers of modest skills who are in search of ideas, designs and sources of inspiration for creating their own projects. The project patterns for the garments in this book are not actual size and should be scaled to suit your requirements.

I have found embroidery to be an uninhibiting and individual form of expression. It evolves from mastering the technique of working the stitches, to creating designs, to — ultimately — completing projects. There are numerous articles you can make; I will be referring to many in this book.

As you will find in the following pages, I use my ideas to formulate a plan which I then work up into a design. Then, once I begin working this design on fabric, I often find that my concept changes and I let my intuition guide me to the desired result.

In a class situation when teaching people ranging from beginners to those of advanced skills, I have found it

INTRODUCTION

beneficial to concentrate on learning and practising a small range of stitches. Once the basics have been mastered, changes in the formation of the stitches and experimentation with threads and colours invariably result in a broader 'vocabulary' of embroidery that can be applied to many different articles.

It is not my purpose to provide a comprehensive guide to stitches in this book. What I aim to do is assist people to develop their unique talents as they explore the rich and rewarding field of creative embroidery.

EMBROIDERY THROUGH THE AGES

In its most rudimentary form, stitchery was employed to join pieces of fabric to make clothing and wall coverings that protected people from the elements. This coarse stitchery evolved into the gentler art of embroidery. Over many centuries, the development of needles made of bone and metal, and the manufacture of a variety of fabrics, have resulted in embroidery becoming increasingly elaborate and intricate.

Embroidery has many applications, both functional and decorative. The appreciation of embroidery as decoration on clothing never seems to diminish.

ACCESSORIES FOR EXCELLENCE

NEEDLES

There are many types of needle available, each suitable for a specific job. When selecting a needle, it is important to consider all the factors that will affect the quality and appearance of the finished work. These will include the thread being used (wool, silk, stranded cotton, silk ribbon, for example) and the fabric on which you will be working.

CREWEL

For fine hand-sewing or embroidery, if a design has been traced or transferred on to fabric, one of the crewel needles is your best choice. These are available in a range of sizes and are sharply pointed.

TAPESTRY

Blunt-ended tapestry needles range in size from 18 to 26. The largest, 18, is usually used with tapestry or coarse types of wool, and is quite thick.

Tapestry No 22 is very useful for embroidery using crewel wool on knitted garments, baby blankets and rugs, and comfortably accommodates between one and four threads. Because of the slight elasticity in crewel wool, No 22 tapestry needle is quite suitable for bullion roses and buds. Even though the eye of the needle is thicker than the shaft (bullion stitch generally calls for a needle that has a shaft and eye of the same thickness) the wool can be drawn through the twists of the stitch and over the eye, and will then ease back into shape.

Tapestry needle No 26 is invaluable in its many applications. It is the finest, shortest tapestry needle and is suitable for cross stitch, ribbon embroidery and embroidery using very fine wools or cottons.

STRAW NEEDLES

These are ideal for bullion stitch. The shaft and the eye of a straw needle are the same thickness and allow the thread to be pulled easily through the twists of the stitch; a standard needle with its eye larger than the shaft would present difficulties for yarns other than crewel wool, as discussed above. The extra length of the straw needle over other needles is advantageous because it allows the thread to be wound round the shaft as many times as necessary to form the desired size of bullion.

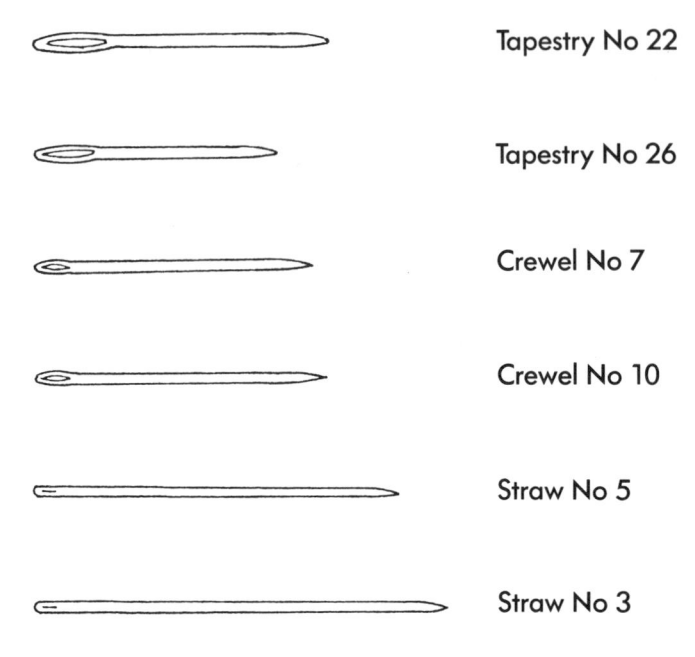

Tapestry No 22

Tapestry No 26

Crewel No 7

Crewel No 10

Straw No 5

Straw No 3

SCISSORS

The importance of using a pair of good-quality scissors can't be understated; they are one of the embroiderer's essential tools.

This author's preference is for the Birch Ultrasharp, a make of scissors that is quite small and extremely light. They are ideal for snipping threads and trimming the back of your work. 'Lift 'n Snip' are also very useful. These are especially good when unpicking stitches, particularly if they have been worked on a knitted garment. These scissors have a curved bottom blade that facilitates the lifting of the thread into the curved cutting area. Only the threads in the curve will be cut, so there will be no mistakes when unpicking or working on delicate areas.

HOOPS

Hoops are available in various materials and in sizes ranging from 3.75 cm (1½ in) to 30 cm (12 in). Cane embroidery hoops have been in use for many years. Both of the rings which form the hoop must be bound to protect the fabric being worked from contact with any rough edges; use bias binding or taffeta ribbon for this purpose.

Spring hoops are a relatively recent innovation and are very popular because they are more quickly secured in place. They are made of moulded plastic and do not need to be bound.

If you are working on a lengthy project, it is advisable to remove the needlework from the hoop when you are not working on it, e.g. after an evening's work on your project, remove the fabric from the hoop. It can become overstretched if left in place for too long, and get soiled around the circumference of the hoop.

THIMBLES

Many people, myself included, prefer to work without a thimble. However, there is a leather thimble with which I feel comfortable. It moulds to the shape of the finger and has an open top; on the underside of the thimble is fitted a small metal disc against which the needle is pressed. A thimble is helpful when using thick fabrics, blunt needles or when working several winds of bullion.

FABRIC AND THREADS

Your selection of fabric should be determined by the type of embroidery, the blend of colours and threads and the effect you wish to achieve with the finished article. As a general rule, a plain fabric is best suited to freestyle embroidery; a textured or patterned fabric may distract from your work and overwhelm the design. A fine voile or batiste that has been machine-embroidered is quite good as a base for embroidery. Stitches can be worked over the cloth design and highlighted with coloured threads.

If you're embellishing a woollen garment, the best threads or wools to use will depend upon the knit. A cable or highly textured effect would not lend itself to the application of stranded cotton, for example, because the embroidered design would disappear into the knit.

Working on a very fine fabric with wools or any of the thicker types of fibre would also be inappropriate. These heavy threads would cause the fabric to pucker and distort.

THREADS

As I have indicated above, threads should be chosen bearing in mind the fabric to be worked and the effect required.

STRANDED COTTON

DMC stranded cotton is of very high quality, and an extensive range of colours is available. This thread comprises six strands which can be used singly, separated into multiples, or used as a whole. Your choice will depend on the type of embroidery and the look you are aiming to achieve.

BRODER COTTON

This is a single-strand thread with a soft sheen. It can be used singly or combined with numerous strands, if desired. I have found this thread exceptionally good for bullion or grub roses, and easy for the novice to handle.

SOFT EMBROIDERY COTTON

Soft embroidery cotton consists of five strands that are loosely twisted and have a matt appearance. Because of its softness, I have found this thread unsuitable for use in single strands. The thread, being so loosely twisted, becomes fluffy if used singly. Used in multiples, it does not present a problem.

MARLITT

Marlitt is 100 per cent polyester. It consists of four threads that can be used singly or in multiples. This is enjoyable to work with for highlighting, outlining, over-embroidery, shadow embroidery and smocking.

KANAGAWA SILK THREAD

This is a relatively new brand of thread which is delightful to use. It is a single, highly twisted strand, and has a lovely sheen. Use in one strand for the best effect because this tends to give a beautiful, smooth, satiny look.

KANAGAWA SILK RIBBON

This silk ribbon gives stitches a natural, almost lifelike appearance. It differs from others because of its softness and ease of manipulation. Other types of ribbon may give a harsher look to embroidery and be more difficult to manage, particularly on finer fabrics.

APPLETONS CREWEL WOOLS

This range is available in a large number of colours, from soft pinks to moss greens and seemingly unlimited shades in between. It is sold in hand-tied skeins of approximately 40 separate strands. Crewel wool is suitable for working singly or in multiple strands, depending on the stitch employed and the appearance that you desire.

HAND-DYED VARIEGATED CREWEL WOOL

This is very similar to Appletons crewel wool, but is hand-dyed so that each strand is in many different shades of the one colour. These wools are available in variegated pinks, green and dusty mauves, among other hues, and are a good alternative to changing colours when you wish to introduce shading within a stitch. They are also useful when needing to complete a project quickly, as you do not have to change wool colours for shading.

TRANSFER METHODS

There is a number of ways in which you can transfer designs from paper onto a garment or other article. Which method you employ will depend on the type of fabric being used and the design you wish to transfer. Listed below are the various methods that I have found effective.

DESIGN OUTLINE IN THREAD

When working on a woollen or knitted garment, tacking the outline of the design into place works well. Use an ordinary sewing thread in a colour that does not feature in the embroidery design.

It is helpful to draw up for yourself a key of basic symbols representing the forms you intend to embroider. For example, I use a large cross for placement of the largest flowers, a smaller cross for smaller flowers, and a continuous tacking stitch to denote trailing or greenery surrounding flowers.

Depending on the design itself, I sometimes prefer to mark the larger shapes and embroider them first, and then to continue with the transfer. This can prove less complicated to the eye, and allows you to assess your progress and make any changes if necessary.

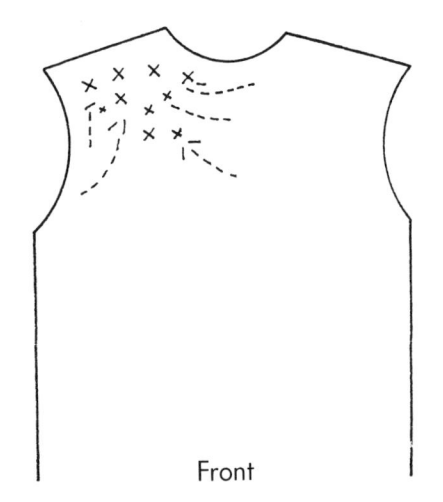

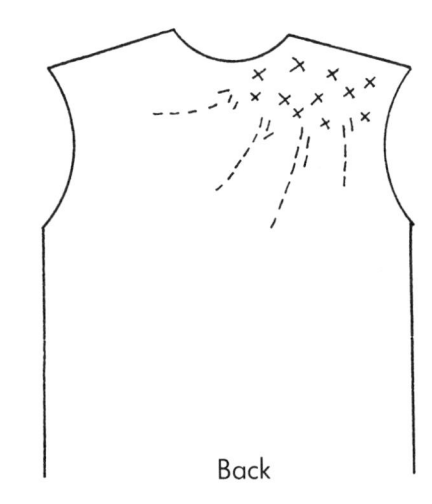

Front

Back

TRANSFER METHODS

IRON-ON TRANSFER PENCIL

A design drawn on paper with these pencils can be transferred on to fabric by the application of heat. You can use your own design or trace over a picture or object you wish to embroider. The pencil lines are transferred to the garment by means of a hot iron. Place a cloth between the paper and the iron to avoid scorching. Hold the iron in place (do not move it about) for 10 to 15 seconds only.

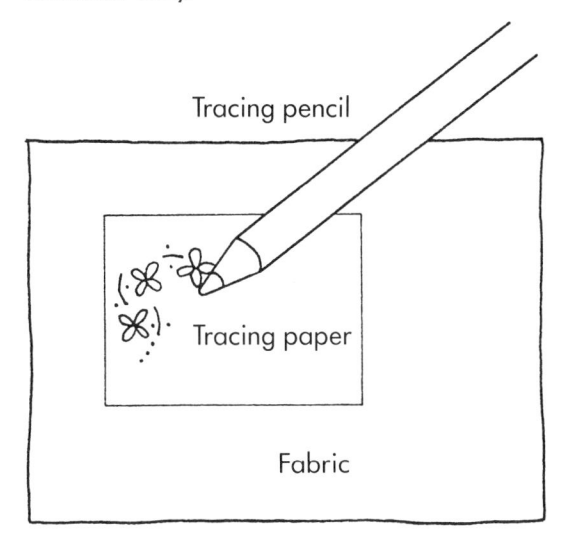

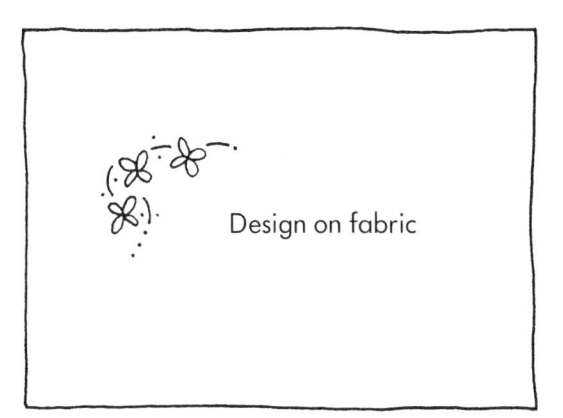

Tracing pencil

Tracing paper

Fabric

Design on fabric

MARKING PENS

These pens temporarily mark fabric. The lines drawn with fast-fade pens usually disappear within 12 to 48 hours. Should you need to remove them sooner, simply apply a moist cloth to the area. Remember to remove all marks before laundering, as some detergents can set the ink. Wash-out marking pens are used in the same way, but to remove marks you must apply a moist cloth because they will not fade automatically.

One type of marking pen has an eraser on one end. Marks should fade within one to 10 days, unless you choose to remove them earlier with the eraser. Both pink and mauve coloured pens are available with erasers; the white one, which is excellent for dark fabrics such as black and navy, does not have an eraser. My experience has shown that these pens work well on many different fabrics including velvet, cotton, organza and woollens.

TRANSFER METHODS

CHALK PAPER

This is used to transfer a design from paper onto a piece of fabric or a garment. First, place the chalk paper on the material, chalk-side down. Second, place the design sheet on top. Then, when you trace the outline with a pencil or other sharply pointed object, the chalk marks will appear on the cloth. The marks will brush off and the paper can be re-used. However, the areas that have already been traced will first have to be reinforced with a chalk pencil.

With finished embroidery

TAILOR'S CHALK

Tailor's chalk is useful in the same way as marking pens. You may need to reinforce the marks made, by using chalk paper or dressmaker's carbon. Chalk marks can be brushed off, or, if more persistent, can be removed by soaking the garment in cold water.

DRESSMAKER'S CARBON

Put the carbon paper in position with the carbon side against the fabric. Place the design on top and trace over it. Take care to outline the design only, or the carbon may smudge on to other areas of the fabric.
Note: Chalk paper and dressmaker's carbon are best suited to smooth fabrics.

A detailed pattern is hard to reproduce on a loosely knitted, soft surface, as pressure must be used on paper/carbon for the pattern to be successfully transferred. Often, the pencil or pointed object will make a hole in the paper or carbon.

STITCHES

Here is a list of the stitches used in the projects in this book. The stitches shown here are represented in simplified symbol form on the design patterns featured in the project section of the book.

Although only a small number of stitches is suggested, each one can be used in many different ways so that its form and effect vary. Simply by using more strands of thread or changing some of the colours, you will have created a completely different look. Another way of changing the design is to experiment with the stitches: instead of using lazy daisy stitch for flowers, see what effect it makes when you use it to embroider leaves and buds. Similarly, use bullion stitches to create forms other than flowers and buds — bunny bodies, for example.

FLOWERS		RUNNING/TRAILING STITCHES	
Bullion Rose		Lazy Daisy	
Bullion Bud		Bullion	
Lazy Daisy		Fly Stitch	
Straight Stitch Rose		Feather Stitch	
Spider's Web Flower		French Knot	
Woven Rose		Straight Stitch	

These particular stitches are varied in their applications and are usually quite quick to embroider. In the designs, I have used all the stitches listed and altered them slightly at times to give more character to the design.

Remember that the more you practise, the more proficient you will become at forming well-shaped stitches. And, when working from the design sheets, feel confident to change the suggested stitch to something you prefer, using the flow of the design as a guide for placement.

If you think that your stitches don't look as uniform and exact as the ones depicted in the diagram, don't despair. Each stitch cannot be a carbon copy of another — I think this variation adds to the individuality of the design. Ten pupils may be given the same project, and choose the same colours and stitches, but each finished interpretation will be quite different — as, indeed, it should be.

FLOWERS

BULLION ROSE

- Insert needle into fabric at point B, then bring needle through fabric to the right side at point A, leaving a short distance between the two points; this represents the length of the finished bullion. You will have formed a large loop with the thread.

  Do not bring the needle all the way through to back of fabric but first insert just the point of the needle through to right side at point A. Bring needle almost all the way through to point A, with only a small part of the eye of the needle remaining in the fabric. The point of the needle and the shaft will be protruding from point A.

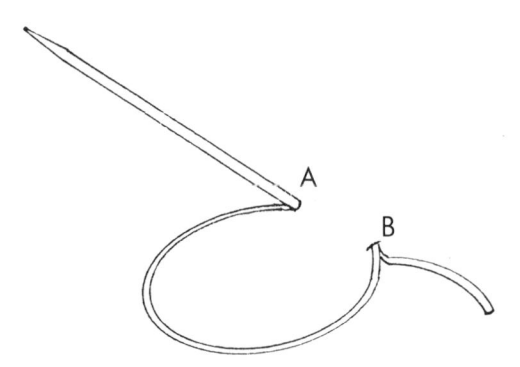

STITCHES

- Twist thread with your finger anti-clockwise around the needle two or three times. If using a tapetry needle with an elongated eye make sure that these twists are wound onto the part of the eye that is protruding from point A. If you are using a straw needle this will not be possible as the eye is small. In this instance, wind the thread onto the shaft, near point A, and push the wrapped thread down onto the eye where it protrudes from point A, before continuing. Continue winding thread around needle a sufficient number of times to cover the length of the bullion.

    Note: I always add two or three extra twists of thread onto the needle; this prevents the bullion from being insufficiently wound to form a full, rounded stitch. Also, when working with a knitted garment, the distance between points A and B (and, therefore, the number of twists needed) can easily be misjudged because of the density of the knit.

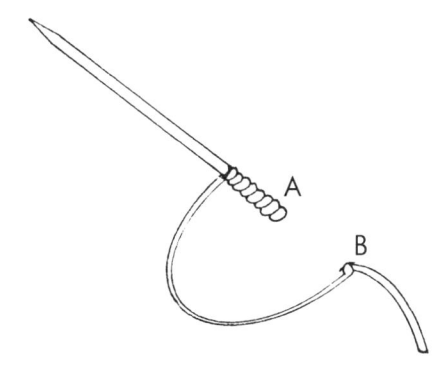

- Hold threads securely with thumb, and gently guide the needle through the twists. Pull the thread firmly, causing bullion to pucker.

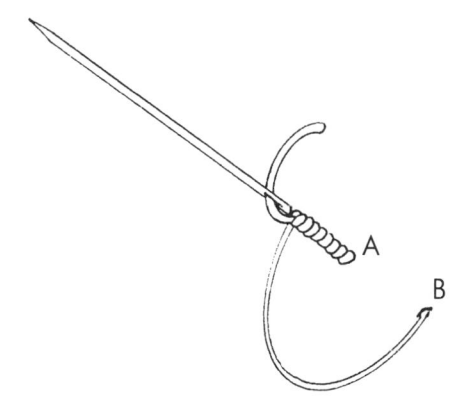

STITCHES

- Pull bullion towards point B, gently ease twists of stitch into place to length required. Insert needle into point B to anchor stitch.

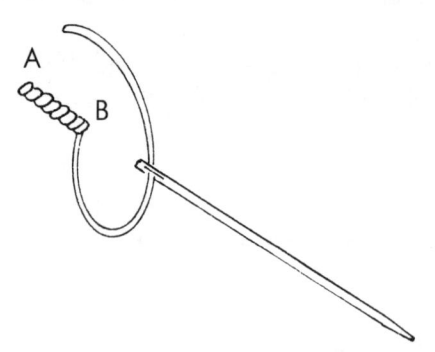

- Continue working centre bullions — two straight bullions as described above will form the centre of the flower.

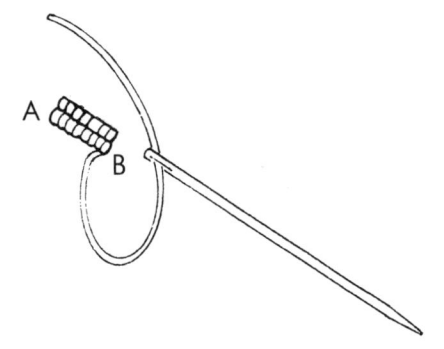

- To begin forming surrounding bullions, bring needle out parallel to the mid-point of the left straight bullion. The curved bullion is then worked so that it encloses the base of the two central straight bullions and extends to a third of the way up the right straight bullion (see diagram).

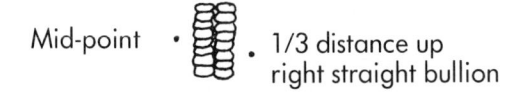

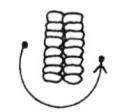

Mid-point · 1/3 distance up right straight bullion

STITCHES

- The next curved bullion begins at the mid-point of the previous one and extends two-thirds of the way up the right straight bullion. Always form the bullions close together, almost bringing the needle from beneath the last bullion stitched.

2/3 distance up
right straight bullion

Mid-point of
previous curved bullion

- Each bullion begins parallel to the mid-point of the previous one, working from the left hand side and continuing around the centre bullions until they are completely encircled. The curved bullions will require a few more wraps than the straight ones that form the centre for them to be properly filled. Continue as shown in following diagram.

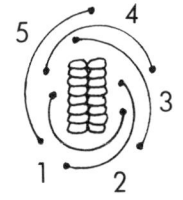

BULLION BUD

Bullion buds are worked in the same way as single bullions. Usually, two single bullions close together are sufficient, but this is a matter of personal choice. The number used will also depend on the fabric used, the threads and the colours.

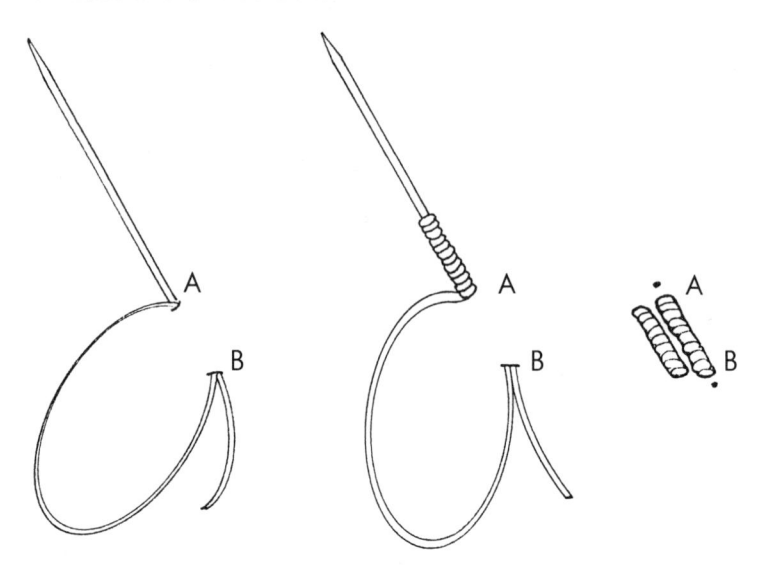

LAZY DAISY

Bring needle through fabric at point A. Hold thread down with your thumb, place needle back in fabric at point B. Bringing needle out of fabric at point C; the distance between point A and point C will be the length of the petal. Draw up the thread, then fasten the loop with a small stitch by inserting the needle into C and bringing it out at point A to start the next stitch, passing onto the wrong side of the work.

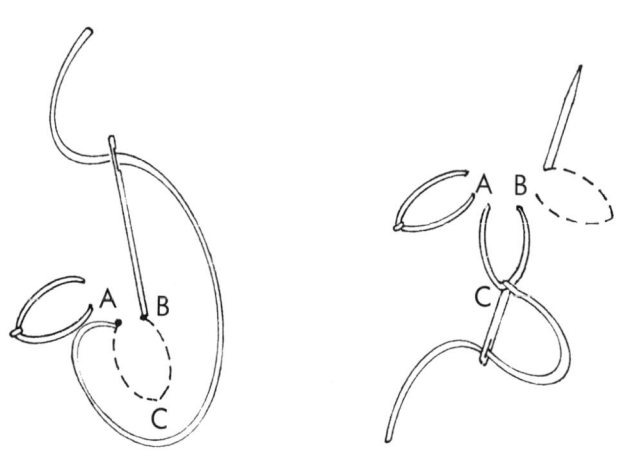

STITCHES

STRAIGHT STITCH ROSE

- Work a square in straight stitches to form the centre of the rose. The amount of stitches will depend on the size of flower required.

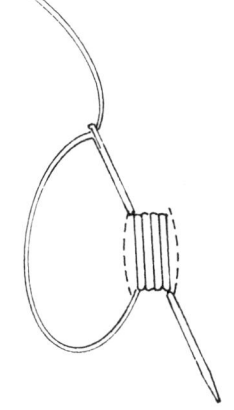

- Begin working straight stitches from point A to point B, covering the corners of the centre straight stitches.

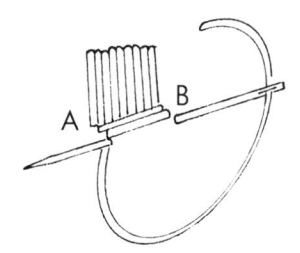

- The third round of colour is worked in the same way as steps A and B. Continue to cover all the corners of the previous round.

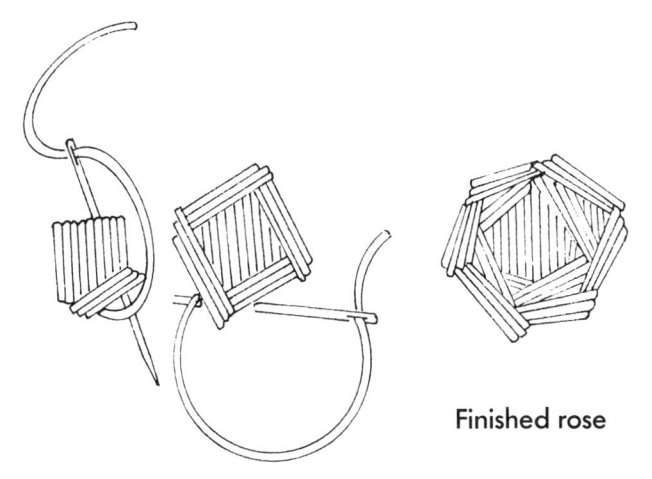

Finished rose

- The final round of stitches needs to be longer than the previous ones. Embroider in the same way as the previous steps.

STITCHES

SPIDER'S WEB FLOWER

The number of 'spokes' for the web can vary, depending on your requirements. Practise by making six single spokes, working from the centre out.

- Bring the needle to the front of the fabric, close to the centre of the web. Working in an anti-clockwise direction, run the needle under two spokes. Loop thread back over second spoke only.
- Take needle under the next two spokes and keep repeating — back over one spoke, forward under two. Continue this procedure until spokes are filled sufficiently to create desired effect.

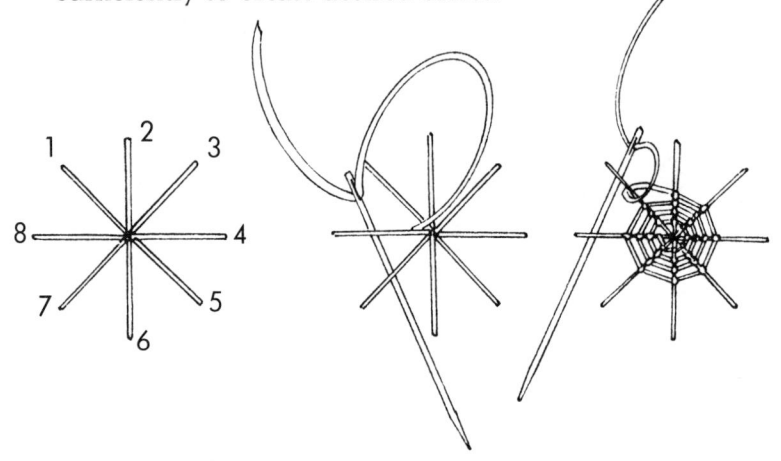

WOVEN ROSE

- To form a woven rose, make an *uneven* number of spokes in the same way as for the spider's web. For the 'weaving', you can use a contrasting thread or one of the same colour. First, bring the needle to the right side of the fabric, close to the centre of the spokes.

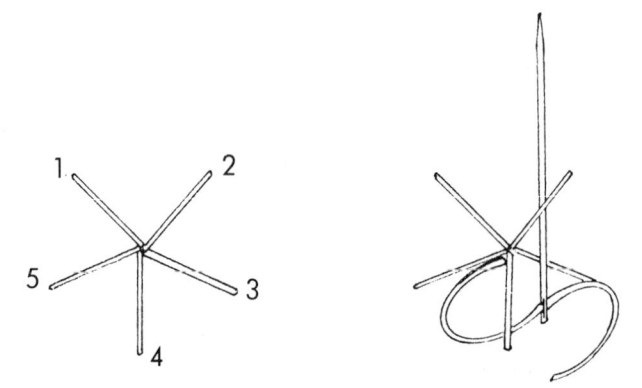

STITCHES

- Working anti-clockwise, weave the thread over and then under the threads, continuing until the full area has been filled in order to achieve the desired result. This is one of the quickest and easiest stitches to work. You can create numerous types of roses with it, the appearance depending on the yarn used, be it cotton, silk ribbon or wool. A French knot may be stitched into the centre as a finishing touch.

  Note: This stitch can only be worked with an uneven number of spokes. If an even number is used, you will be weaving over and under the same spokes. This will not give the appearance of a properly woven flower.

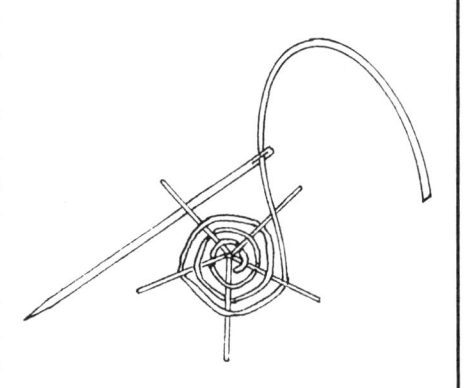

RUNNING/TRAILING STITCHES

LAZY DAISY

To form running stitches with lazy daisy, simply stitch single petals in a sequence. Three petals together can look effective around flowers.

BULLION

Single bullions (made as described in the Flowers section) can be grouped as surrounds for rose buds, worked into leaves for large flowers, or sewn in pairs to form a V-shape as greenery.

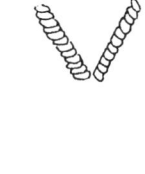

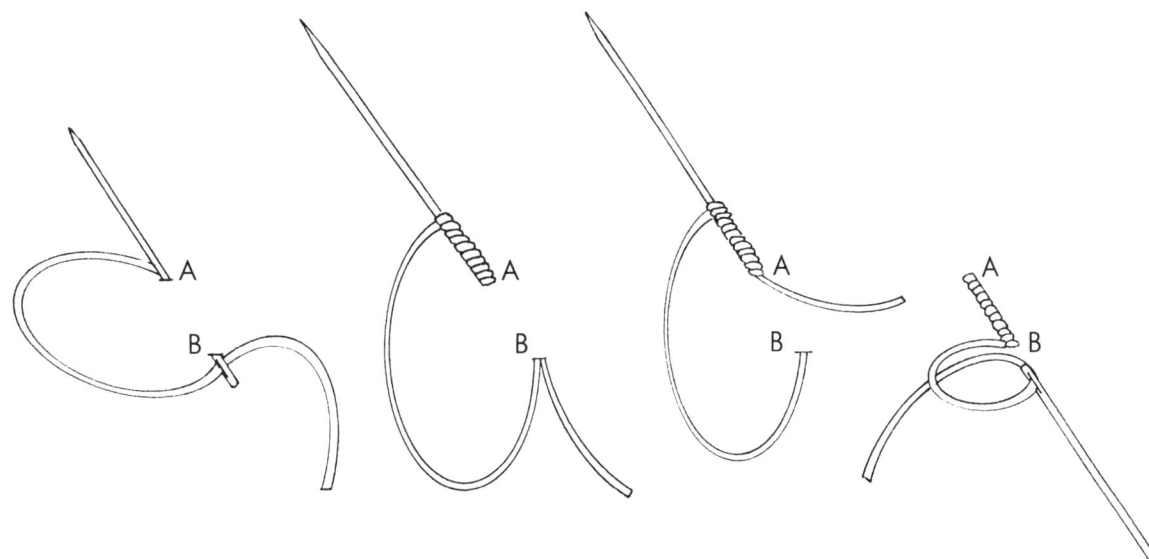

STITCHES

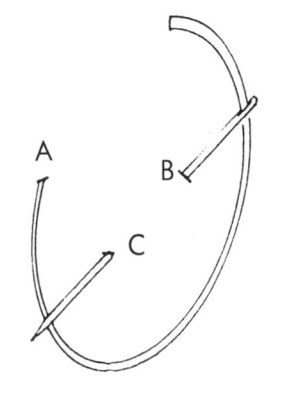

FLY STITCH

Bring needle through fabric at point A. Hold thread down with your thumb, place needle back into fabric at point B, bring needle out at point C, taking it through to the back of the work to secure thread to form a V-shape.

Form a double fly stitch by stitching a second smaller V-shape from C to D, below A and B, before securing both stitches with a single long straight stitch from E to F.

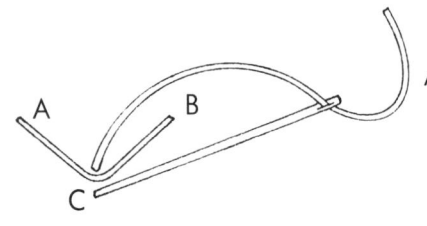

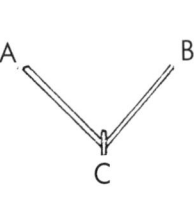

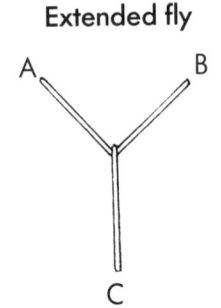

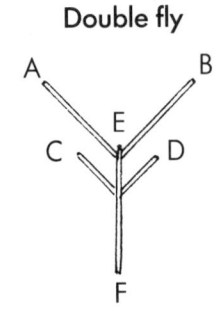

EXTENDED FLY STITCH

To form an extended fly stitch, form a single fly stitch as described above, increasing the length of the final straight stitch to represent a stem, or, on large-scale designs, continuous greenery.

FEATHER STITCH

The stitch is begun in the same way as fly stitch. Each fly stitch is linked to the next, forming a trail of soft 'U' shapes. This stitch is good for trailing between flowers, or as the stems for a bunch of flowers. It is also useful as a border stitch around the neck or cuff of a garment. Use it, too, as a 'link' for a trailing floral design.

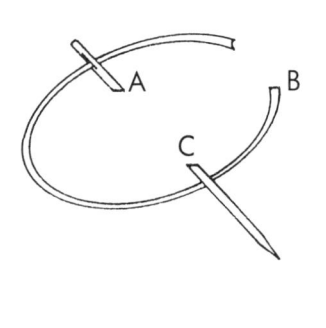

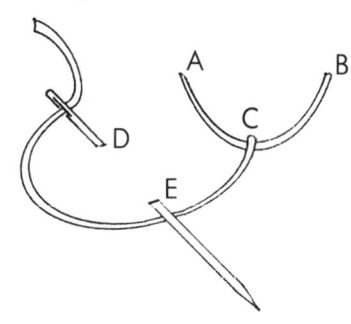

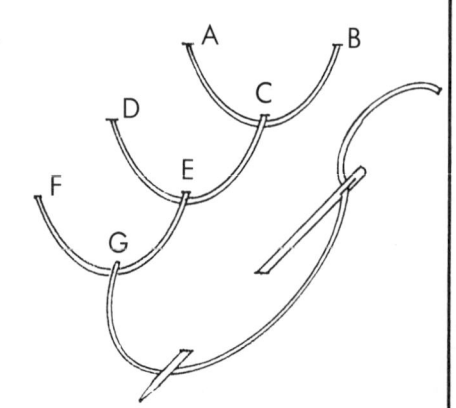

FRENCH KNOT

Bring needle through to the right side of fabric, hold the thread with free hand and wrap it around the needle once or twice. Insert the point of needle close to the starting point (1-2 mm away), then pull thread tight. Pull needle through fabric, leaving knot of required height on the surface.

French knots can be made using several threads, or by using more than one or two winds around the needle.

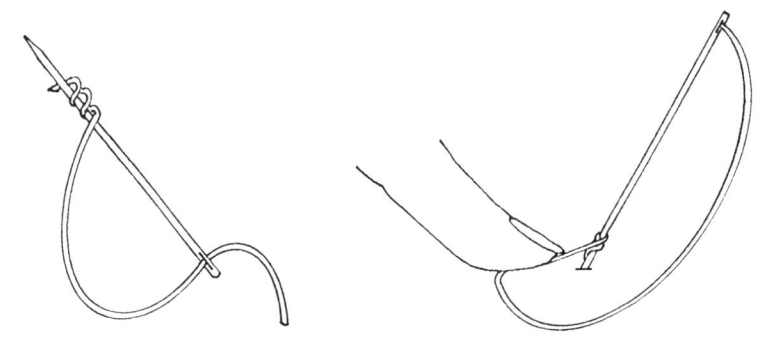

STRAIGHT STITCH

Surely, the simplest of all stitches! Bring the needle to the right side of the fabric at point A. Depending on the length of the stitch required, insert needle into the fabric at point B. It is a good idea to keep these stitches to a moderate length; if they are too long, they may look loose. They could catch on jewellery if the design is worked onto a garment.

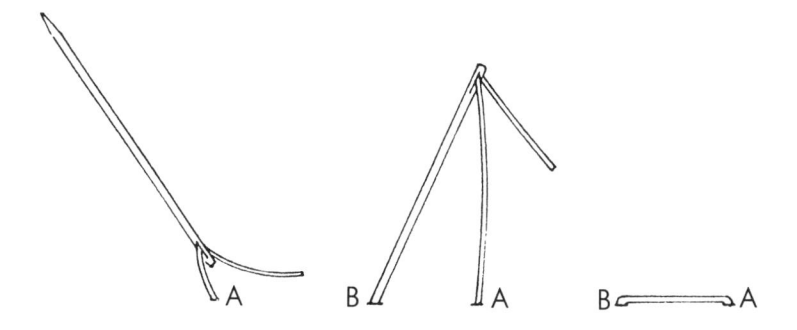

DESIGN CONSIDERATIONS

ADAPTING STITCHES TO DESIGNS

A stitch does not have only a single function to fulfil. It can be used in many different situations in a design so that you can 'paint' the picture you want. As you will notice when looking at my embroidered articles in this book, I regularly vary the use of a certain stitch to add character and detail to my work. For example, lazy daisies are suitable not only for working flowers, but for a trail of greenery. Single bullions can be embroidered in green to surround rose buds; extended-stem fly stitch works well for leaves around roses and buds.

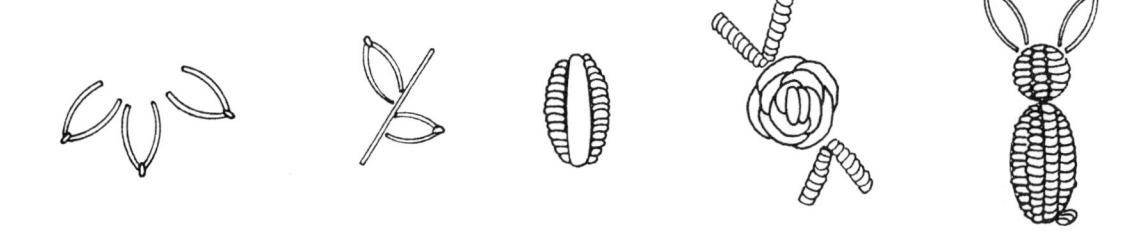

CREATING A DESIGN

Free-style embroidery evolves from one's individual style and interpretation of the design. The way in which you mass the stitches into a formation is entirely of your own making..

Let the stitches be created with the help of your imagination. Often, your first idea will be the best, so let intuition be your guide.

Many factors will play a part in determining the type of design you create: your selection of colour, fabric and thread is of great significance in deciding what you will be aiming for. It would not be suitable, for instance, to work a large design with wools onto delicate voile or organza. Similarly, it would be inappropriate to work a single thread of stranded cotton onto a coarse-knit woollen jumper.

Most importantly, remember that your imagination can be both a liberating and a restricting factor. Allow your imagination to run free.

HELPFUL HINTS

1. I find it helpful to have a sketch pad on hand when beginning to work on a project. You can jot down ideas, details of the way in which you have used stitches, colour numbers and amount of thread required, for example.

2. After working a stitch, be sure to let the needle drop from the cloth so that the threads can untwist. This will make the next stitch easier to work, and help to give it an even, precise look.

3. When working bullion stitches, it is particularly important to remember to let the thread untwist. Because you are winding the threads around the needle to form the bullion, it is necessary to reverse the process before commencing work on the next stitch.

4. When using a single strand of thread for bullion stitch, always make sure that the threads wound around the needle are lying flat. This will ensure the formation of a smooth bullion.

5. Pull the needle almost all the way through the cloth, leaving only the eye concealed when working bullion. In the case of a tapestry needle, because it has an elongated eye, you will be able to wind the thread onto the part of the eye protruding through the fabric. If using a straw needle, which has a small eye, it will not be possible to use this method, so wrap the thread around the shaft.

6. If a hole is made in the fabric accidentally while unpicking a stitch, gently place the fibres back in place. A substance called Fray check/Fray stoppa is a liquidised plastic that is transparent when dry. It seals cut areas by bonding the fibres together again.

7. Always weave threads moderately loosely between stitches at the back of a knitted garment to allow for stretch and movement with wear.

8. You may sometimes find it easier to iron Marlitt threads before use. Place a cloth over the threads and press with a steam-iron. This will remove the folds that form in the skein.

HELPFUL HINTS

9. If you are using a straw needle with more than one strand of thread, try threading the needle with two or three of the threads first. Then thread the remainder into the eye of the needle. I find this method much easier than fiddling with numerous threads all at the one time.

10. If you are having difficulty threading the needle, try drawing the thread across a bar of soap which is just damp. This will enable the threads to slip through the needle with ease. Trim off the moist ends before beginning to stitch.

11. When threading wool into a tapestry needle, loop the wool over the eye of the needle, pull it tight, draw the needle out and then thread looped wool into the eye.

12. Some fabrics have a nap or pile. This means that the cloth may feel smooth when your hand brushes across it in one direction, and rough when your hand brushes it the other way. Also, the cloth may look matt from a certain angle, and shiny when looked at from a different aspect.

13. If you need to complete an embroidery project quickly, use a variegated thread or wool. This will save you having to change colours as frequently as would be necessary with a single-shade thread.

14. I find it beneficial to take the time and trouble to experiment with threads and colours when planning a project. With so much to choose from, the decision is important and should be carefully considered.

15. Keep your hands smooth. Rough skin is a particular drawback when working with Marlitt thread as the yarn will catch and stitching will become difficult.

16. If you are having trouble pulling a needle through a thick piece of fabric, try using a needle grabber. This is a small piece of rubber designed to help you get a grip on the needle.

17. Always embroider in a good light, with no shadow falling on your work. A lamp directed at the embroidery is a must in the evenings; try to use a daylight blue-light globe. A magnifying lamp is a very helpful accessory; it not only allows you to see your work as clearly as possible, it also magnifies it for easier stitching.

18. Soft embroidery cotton must always be used in

multiples. It does not work in a single strand because the thread is so loosely twisted and soft.

19. Broder cotton is one of the easiest threads to use when working bullions. This is a single strand, quite highly twisted thread with a soft sheen. I recommend this to beginners wishing to experiment and achieve a good result with bullion without wearing out their patience.

20. Often, your first idea is the best. Jot it down so that you can return to it after exploring other possibilities.

PROJECTS AND DESIGNS

BABY'S NAVY KNIT JUMPER AND LEGGINGS

This is a commercially made garment in pure wool and is fully machine washable; this is important for a baby's or child's garment. I chose to work with the hand-dyed variegated crewel wools. They produce a most unusual effect — a mixture of colours within the one stitch formation. It is quicker to work a design with these yarns because you don't have to use two or three different shades and, therefore, change yarns, to complete a single flower. The leggings are also commercially made and are of pure wool. These two garments make a lovely set for a child, or are equally attractive as individual pieces.

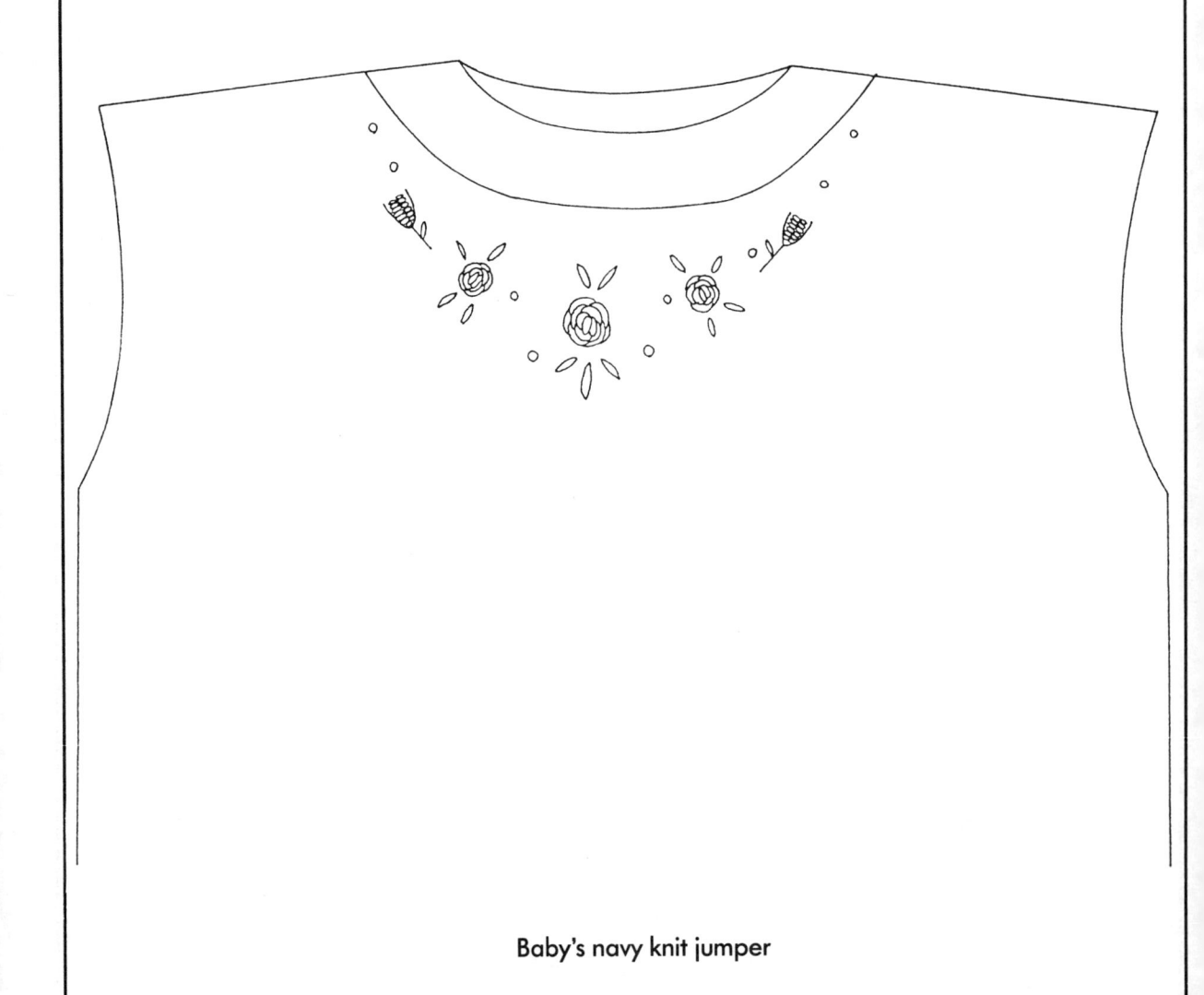

Baby's navy knit jumper

PROJECTS AND DESIGNS

Feet of baby's navy leggings

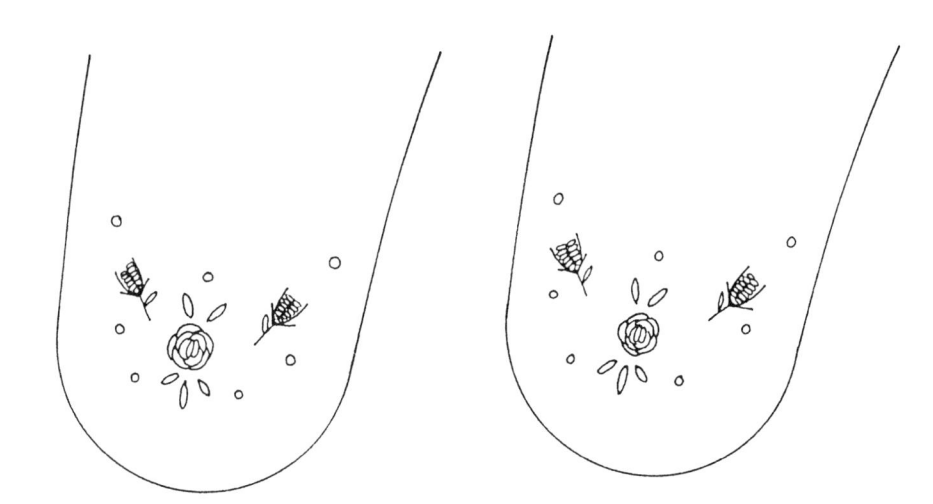

STITCHES

Bullion Rose
Bullion Bud
Lazy Daisy
French Knot
Double Fly

COLOURS

A — Variegated pink
B — Variegated green

Appletons crewel wool:
D — 711 Light dusty pink

STITCH COLOURS

Bullion Rose: A — V/pink
Bullion Bud: A — V/pink
Double Fly: B — V/green
French Knot: D — 711
Lazy Daisy: B — V/green

STITCH FORMATION

Bullion roses and buds are worked in variegated pink (A), using two strands. Green around flowers and buds is worked with one strand of variegated green (B), using lazy daisy stitches to form the leaves. French knots are stitched with Appletons crewel wool, D — 711, using one strand wrapped twice around needle. A No 22 tapestry needle is suitable with this wool.

Leggings are worked with the same threads. First, work a bullion rose in the centre of the top of each foot, then a bullion bud to each side. These flowers are then surrounded with B — V/green, using lazy daisy stitch and double fly stitch with one strand of thread.

PROJECTS AND DESIGNS

DETACHABLE YOKE FOR BABY'S GARMENT

A baby's two-piece, knitted suit (size 00) consisting of a short-sleeved top and a pair of pants was purchased for this design. The buttons on the shoulder allow the yolk to be removed, leaving the garment plain. The yoke can be buttoned onto another garment such as a T-shirt, dress, romper suit or jumper.

STITCHES

Bullion
Lazy Daisy
French Knot
Straight Stitch

COLOURS

All DMC stranded cotton
   A2 — 210 Mauve
   B2 — 445 Pale yellow
   C2 — 800 Soft blue
   I — 504 Green
   V — 754 Pale apricot
   Y — 318 Grey
   Z — 963 Pink
   D2 — 317 Dark Grey

STITCH COLOURS

Bullion and Lazy Daisy:
   Y — 318
   D2 — 317

French Knots:
   A2 — 210
   B2 — 445
   C2 — 800
   V — 754
   Z — 963

Straight Stitch:
   I — 504

STITCH FORMATION

Bullions are stitched first to form the bunnies' bodies and heads. Use four threads of DMC stranded cotton, Y — 318 and D2 — 317. The ears of the smaller bunnies are formed using lazy daisy stitch, with one strand. The inner ears are in straight stitch using one strand of Z — 963. The ears of the larger bunnies are formed using lazy daisy stitch with one strand of Y — 318. Inner ears are the same as for the small bunnies.

PROJECTS AND DESIGNS

Grass and flower stems are embroidered in straight stitch with one strand of I — 504. French knots are used to create the flowers. Use A2 — 210, B2 — 445, C2 — 800, V — 754 and Z — 963, each in a single strand. French knots around scalloped edge of yoke are in I — 504 and Z — 963, also using one strand.

The eyes of the bunnies are made with French knots, using a single strand of D2 — 317.

The butterfly is worked with one strand of B2 — 445. Wings and body are in lazy daisy stitch. A French knot using one strand Z — 963 is worked for the head.

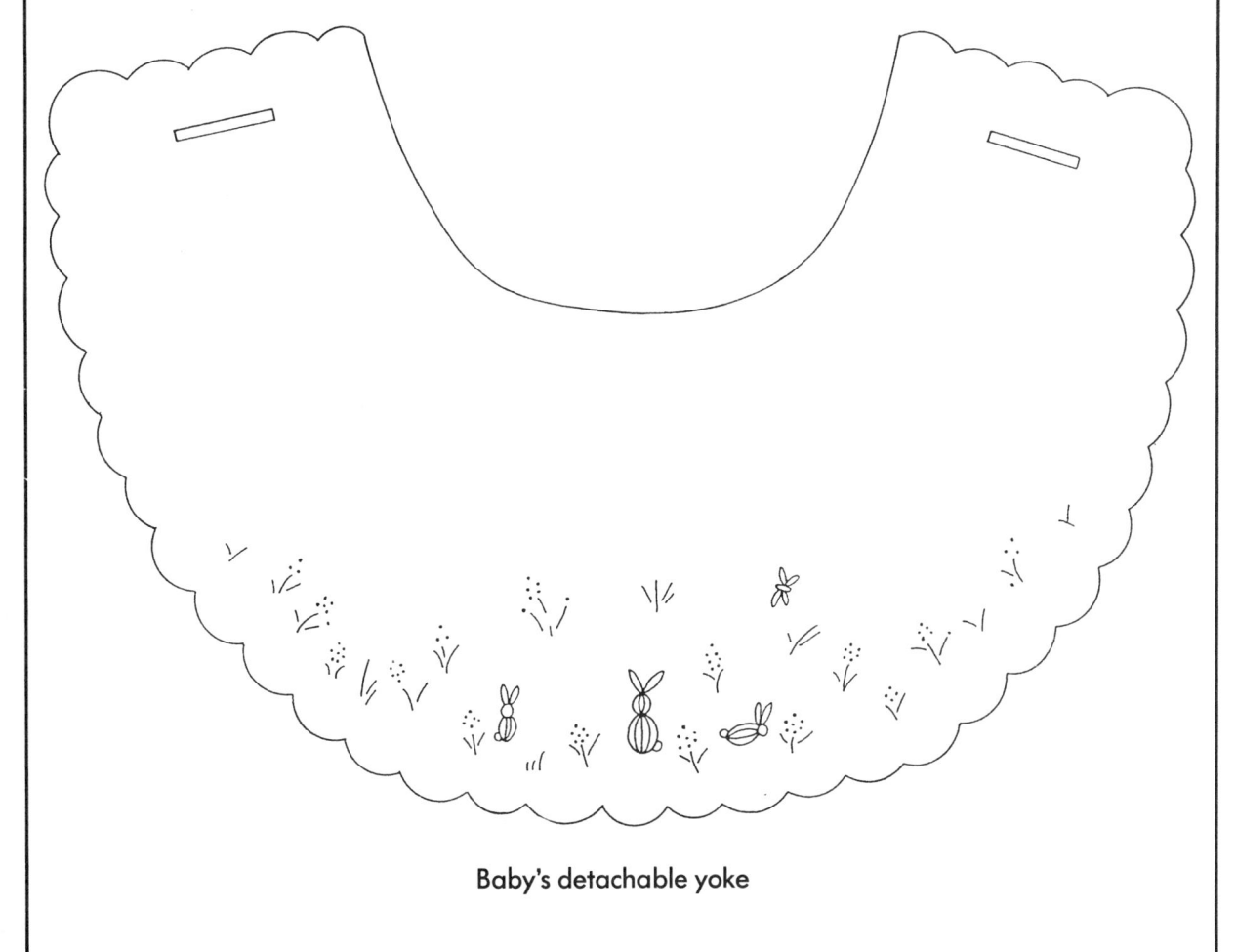

Baby's detachable yoke

PROJECTS AND DESIGNS

BABY'S COTTON BLANKET

A baby's blanket in white cotton is required for this project. I chose to use Appletons crewel wools for this design. The softness of the blanket and the wools complemented its simplicity and effectiveness. Medici (DMC) wool — a very fine single strand, quite suitable for embroidery — is used to stitch the French knots in the centres of the lazy daisy flowers.

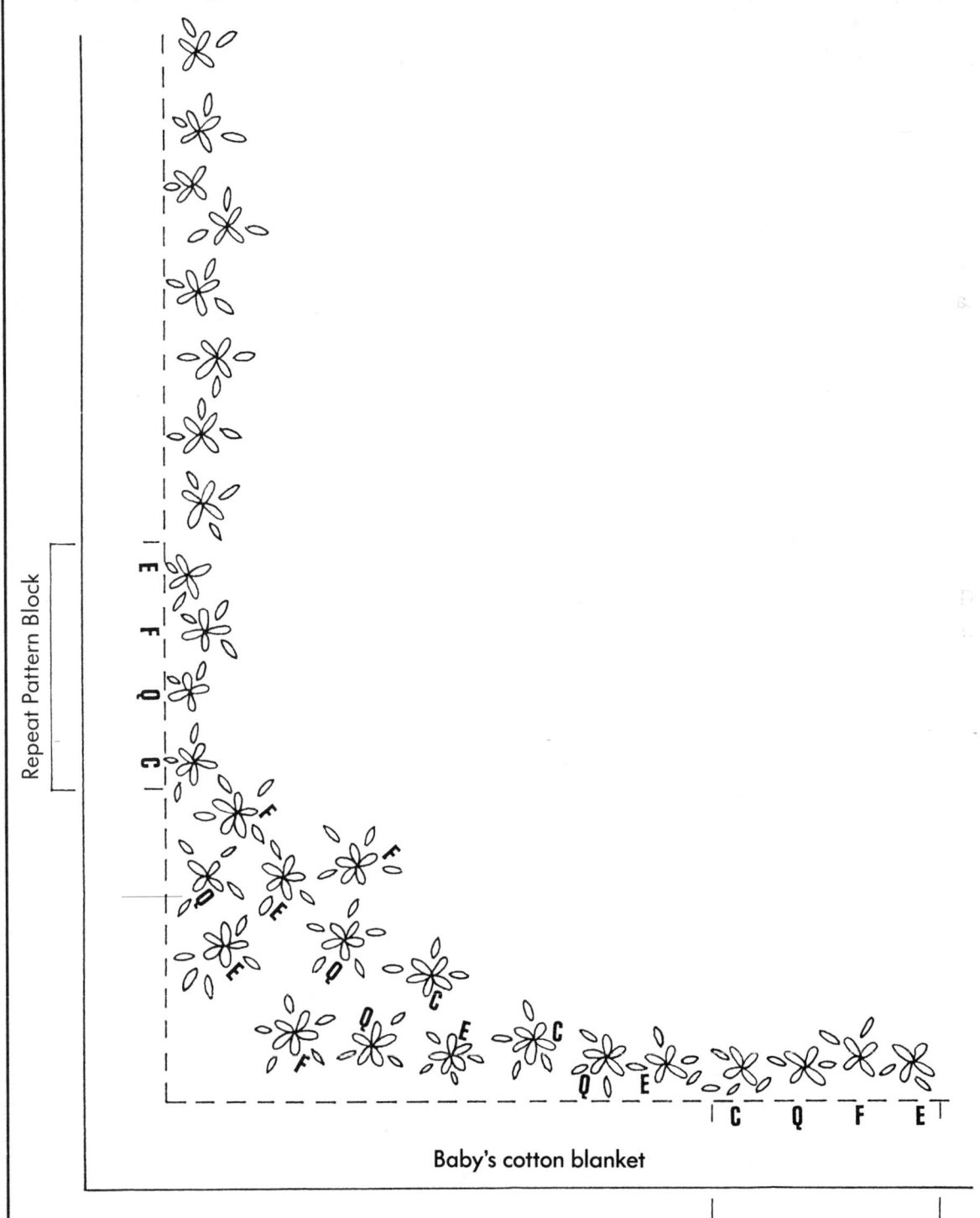

Baby's cotton blanket

Repeat Pattern Block

STITCHES

Lazy Daisy
French Knot

COLOURS

Appletons crewel wool
- C — 712 Light dusty pink
- D — 711 Lightest dusty pink
- E — 741 Cornflour blue
- F — 601 Light mauve
- Q — 223 Pale apricot
- K — 356 Mid green

8327 — DMC Medici wool

STITCH COLOURS

Lazy Daisy:
- C — 712
- D — 711
- E — 741
- F — 601
- Q — 223
- K — 356

French Knots:
8327 (Buttercup) — Medici (DMC)

STITCH FORMATIONS

First, the larger lazy daisies are stitched into the corners of the blanket, following the pattern of colour depicted on the design sheet. Continue working around the edges of the blanket in the sequence of C — 712; Q — 223; F — 601; E — 741. Use one strand of Appletons crewel wool for all lazy daisy stitches. Use Medici DMC 8327 for the French knots in the centres of the lazy daisy flowers.

Greenery is stitched using K — 356. The leaves are formed by single lazy daisy petals, placed where appropriate.

Note: It is more practical to trail the thread between flowers, gently weaving into the back of the blanket to secure threads and stitches. Be careful not to let any of the weaving show on the right side of the blanket.

PROJECTS AND DESIGNS

DRESSING TABLE SET, BROOCH AND GLOVES

The beautiful soft texture of the ivory-coloured velvet chosen for this project made working the design a delight. To keep the embroidery design delicate necessitated using a single strand of Kanagawa silk thread. Soft shades of peach and green were used to complement the ivory velvet.

The brooch and dressing-table set are Framecraft products which are of very high quality. I chose the gold set because it went well with the colour of the velvet. The clothes brush is also a Framecraft product.

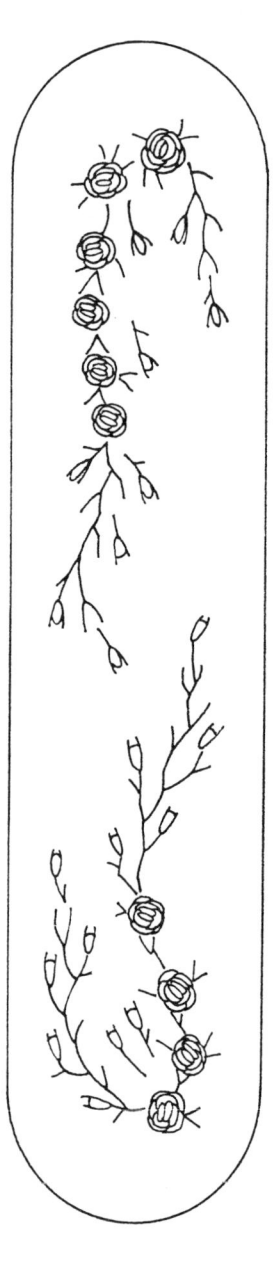

Dressing table set:
Clothes brush

STITCHES

Bullion Rose
Bullion Bud
Fly Stitch
Feather Stitch
Lazy Daisy

COLOURS

All Kanagawa pure silk thread
   L — 825 Medium peach
   M — 94 Light peach
   R — 827 Fern green

STITCH COLOURS

Bullion Rose:
   L — 825 (centres)
   M — 94 (surround)

Bullion Bud:
   L — 825
   M — 94

Fly and Feather Stitch:
   R — 827

Lazy Daisy:
   R — 827

STITCH FORMATION

The centres of all the bullions are stitched using a single strand of silk, L — 825. The surrounding bullions are worked using M — 94, also in a single strand, as are the bullion buds.

First mark the design on all the objects using an erasable marking pen. Then embroider the feather stitches (in a single strand) on all the items. This gives you a trail to follow for placement of bullion roses and buds. Fly stitch and lazy daisy are also worked in a single strand.

PROJECTS AND DESIGNS

Note: It is important to cut the fabric larger than the dimension of the mirror, brush, clothes brush and brooch because each of these items is padded. The fabric must be of sufficient size to cover the padded area and then be secured in place.

I usually place some Fray check/Fray stoppa around all the cut areas of the fabric. This liquid plastic hardens slightly when dry and prevents edges from fraying.

It is also important to remember that velvet has a nap. This should be taken into account when placing the design on the cloth.

Left hand glove   Right hand glove

PROJECTS AND DESIGNS

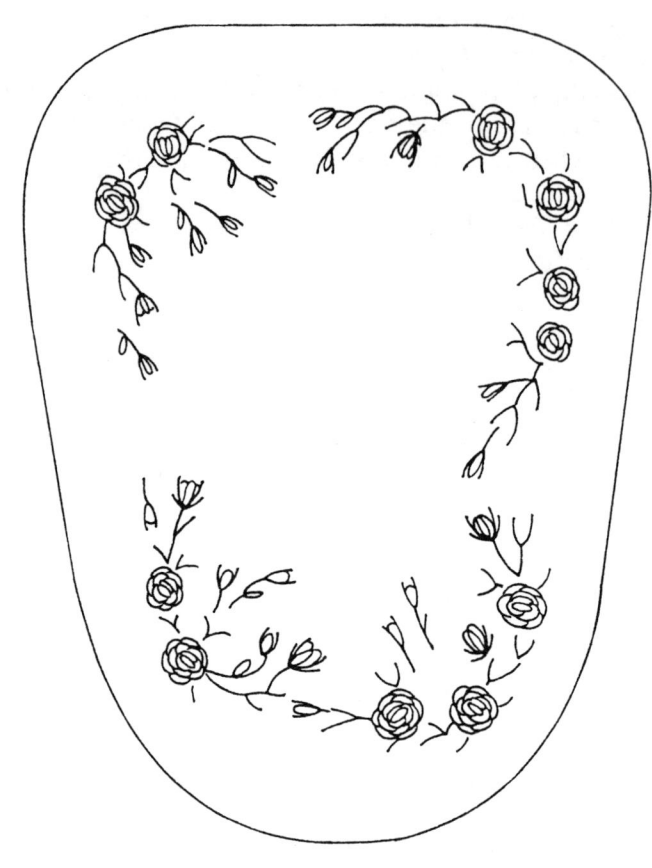

Dressing table set:
Brush

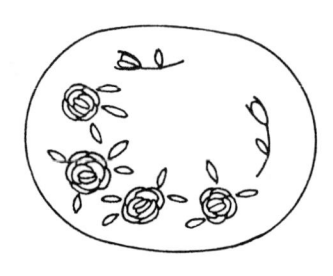

Brooch

PROJECTS AND DESIGNS

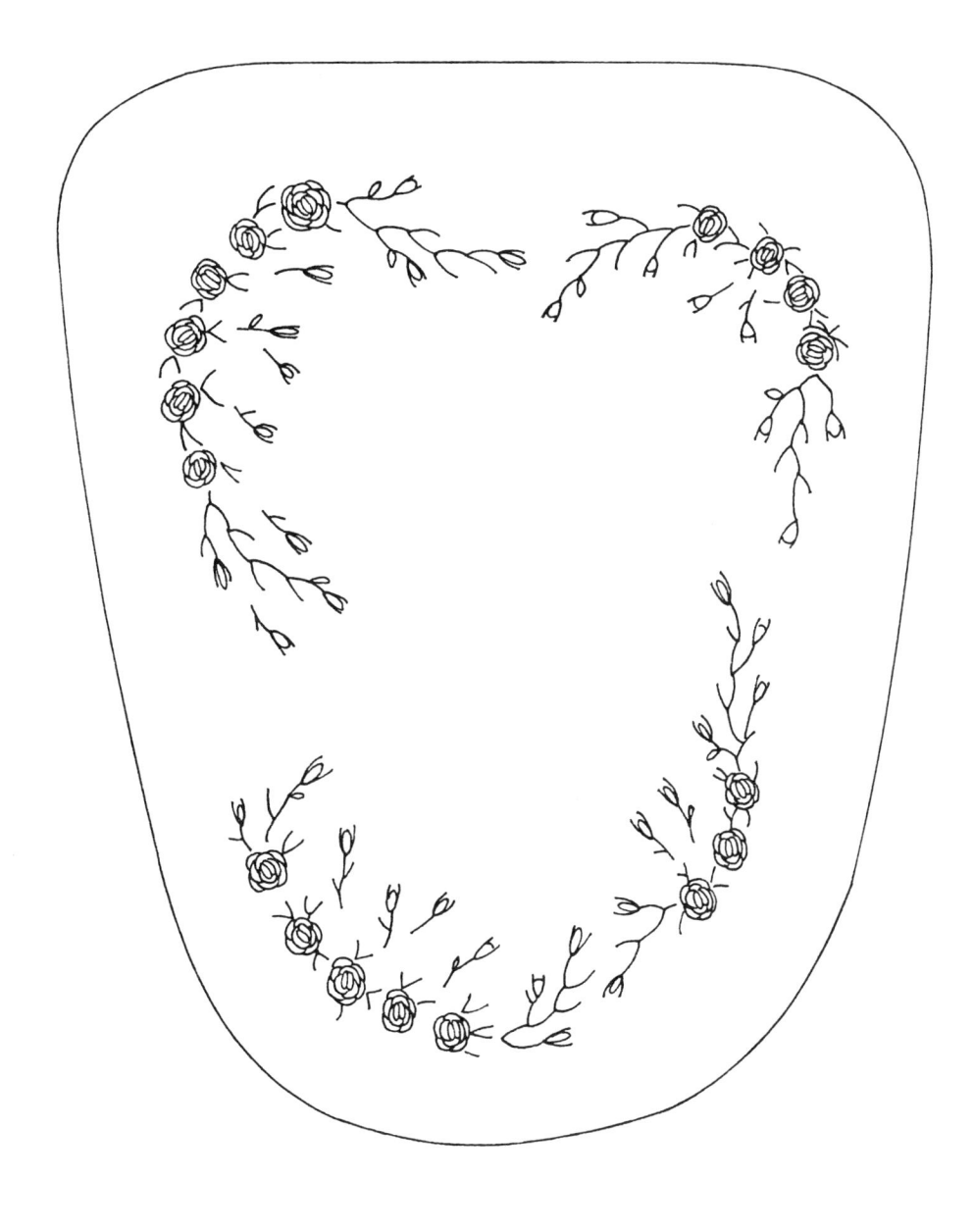

Dressing table set:
Mirror

PROJECTS AND DESIGNS

GRANDMA'S HOUSE TRINKET POT

I painted and stitched the trinket pot illustrated in the colour section as a memento of my grandparents. I recollect that their home was a lived-in, hospitable place which saw many changes between the 1930s and 1970s while their nine children were raised and grew up. Any house or subject of your choice can be painted and stitched on to cloth this way, employing your own colour and stitch selection.

French Knot
Straight Stitch
Fly Stitch

COLOURS

All DMC stranded cotton
    E2 — 340 Mauve
    F2 — 776 Pink
    G — 502 Green
    G2 — 840 Brown
    H2 — 932 Blue
    K — 761 Pink
    P — 320 Green
    V — 754 Flesh colour

STITCH COLOURS

French Knots:
    G — 502
    P — 320
    K — 761
    H2 — 932
    E2 — 340
    F2 — 776

Straight Stitch:
    G2 — 840
    V — 754

Fly Stitch:
    P — 320

STITCH FORMATION

Using a pencil, draw an outline to indicate the shape of the house on the cloth you have chosen. Using watercolour paints, test them on a spare piece of cloth, the same as that to be used for the trinket pot, to determine their strength and colour. Make sure the cloth used for the embroidery is moistened, and your brush

BABY'S THINGS
Baby's cotton blanket; baby's jumper and leggings; detachable yoke

DRESSING TABLE SET, BROOCH, GLOVES AND GRANDMA'S HOUSE – TRINKET POT

NAVY KNIT CARDIGAN

SOFT-PINK KNIT JUMPER

CREAM KNIT JUMPER

Navy Cotton-Knit Jumper

Black Fine-Knit Jumper

is wet. Begin by painting the sky (I used a very soft blue), then paint the ground around the house (I chose earth brown). Using a smaller brush, begin painting the house (I selected a red-brown to achieve a realistic depiction of the home). Take a fine fabric-marker and outline the house, and draw an outline of a tree and fence (I used brown in all instances, with green for the leaves). Leave the cloth to dry completely before you commence the embroidery.

Use a single strand of thread for the stitches in this piece. Start with the roof, using straight stitch in G2 — 840. Stitch the wisteria around the verandah posts and along the verandah using E2 — 340 and F2 — 776. Embroider the grass along the fence and in front of the house in fly stitch using P — 320.

Using V — 754, insert the single straight stitch between the green of the fly stitch. Then place French knots along the fence and front of the house, alternating H2 — 932 and K — 761. The path is partly stitched using straight stitches in G2 — 840.

Form the leaves in the tree in French knots, using mainly P — 320 and some G — 502.

PROJECTS AND DESIGNS

WHITE CARDIGAN

(As shown on front cover)

A fine machine-knit cotton cardigan was used for this project. I find that perfectly plain garments or fabrics allow for more creativity within the design, and give greater impact to the embroidery.

This cardigan fastens to the neck with self-covered buttons. I chose soft colours and a few simple stitches to complement this garment.

STITCHES

Bullion Rose
Bullion Bud
Lazy Daisy
Fly Stitch
French Knot

COLOURS

DMC Broder cotton No 16
    A — 818 Light pink
    B — 776 Medium pink
    E — 745 Buttercup

DMC stranded cotton
    I2 — 523 Green

STITCH COLOURS

Bullion Rose:
    A — 818 (surround)
    B — 776 (centres)

Bullion Bud:
    A — 818
    B — 776

French Knot:
    E — 745

Lazy Daisy:
    I2 — 523

Fly Stitch:
    I2 — 523

STITCH FORMATION

I began working this design by stitching a guide with sewing thread to indicate where the embroidery stitches were to be placed.

Centres of bullion roses are worked using two threads of broder cotton B — 776; twist thread around the needle as many times as necessary to complete the length of bullion. Surrounding bullions to form rose petals have been stitched using two strands of A — 818. Bullion buds also use two strands of thread.

Greenery around roses and buds is in I2 — 523 using two strands; use fly stitch and lazy daisy. French knots use one thread only of E — 745 once around the needle.

Note: Use a straw needle No 3 for bullions and buds, and a tapestry needle No 26 for fly stitch, lazy daisy and French knots.

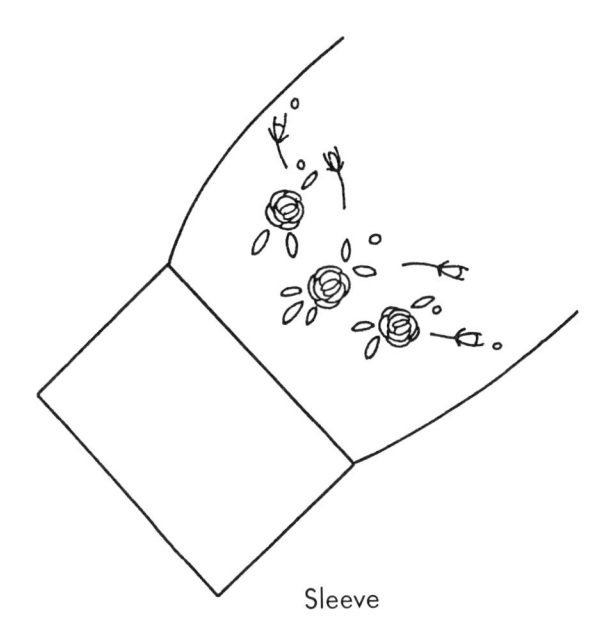

Sleeve

PROJECTS AND DESIGNS

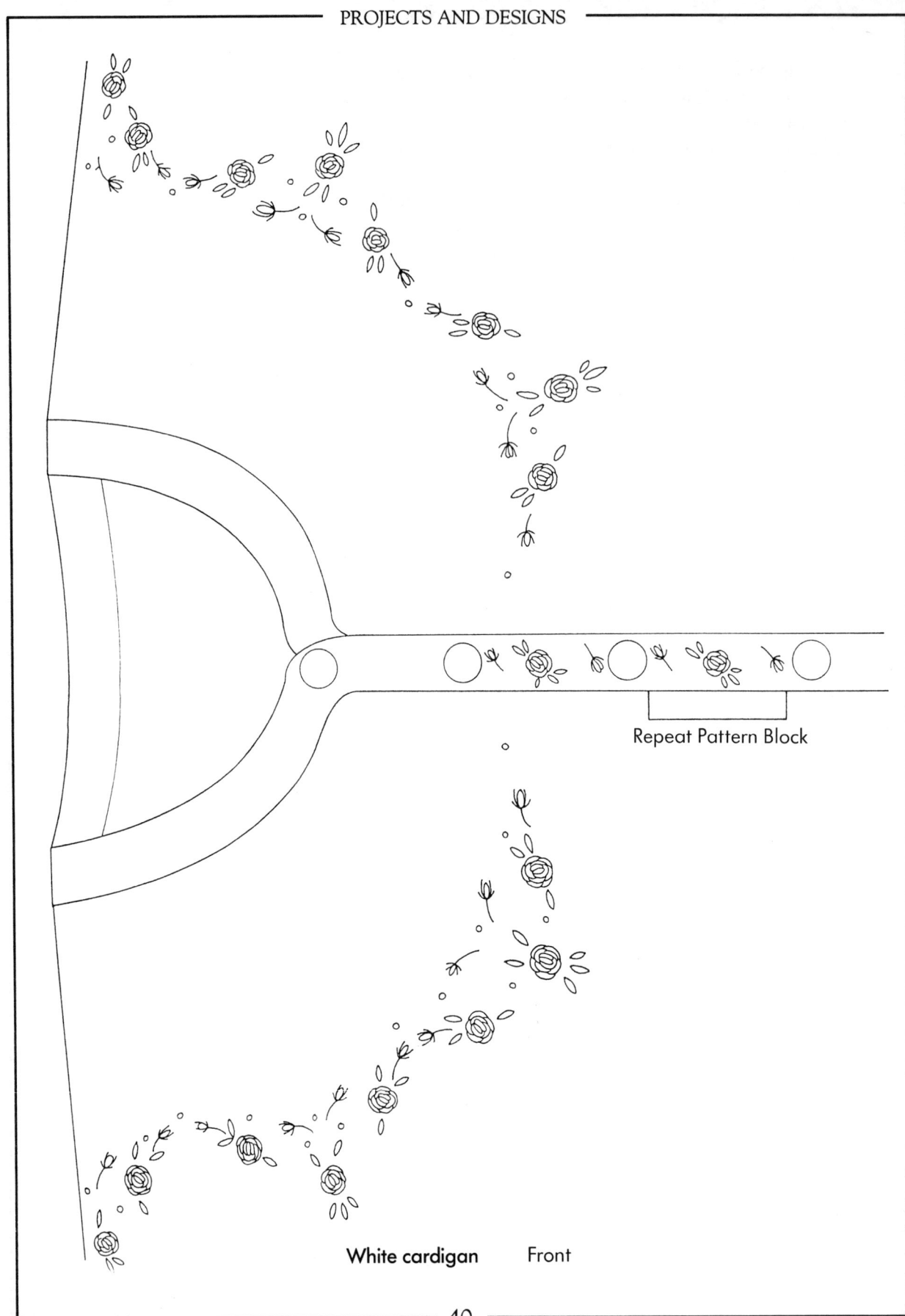

Repeat Pattern Block

White cardigan   Front

PROJECTS AND DESIGNS

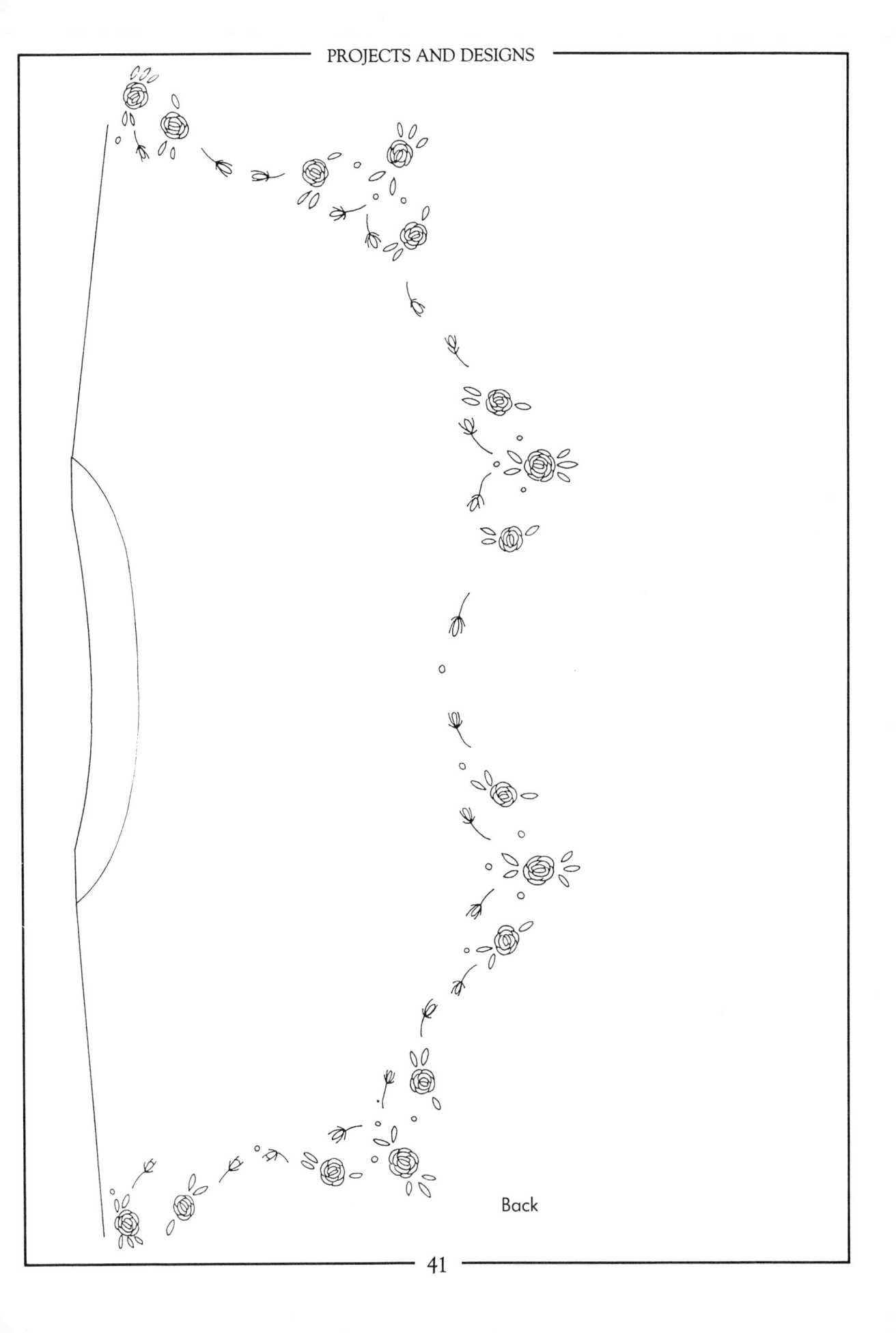

Back

41

PROJECTS AND DESIGNS

NAVY KNIT CARDIGAN

The design worked on this knitted cardigan has been stitched in Appletons crewel wools in a variety of soft dusky pinks and greens. This garment has extra-wide cuffs, drop shoulders and is a long length.

STITCHES

Bullion Rose
Bullion Bud
Lazy Daisy
Spider's Web
Fly Stitch
French Knot

COLOURS

All Appletons crewel wool
A — 714 Dark dusty pink
B — 713 Medium dusty pink
C — 712 Light dusty pink
J — 354 Medium green
K — 356 Mid/Dark green

STITCH COLOURS

Bullion Rose:
  A — 714 (centres)
  B — 713 (1st surrounds)
  C — 712 (2nd surrounds)

Bullion Bud:
  A — 714
  B — 713
  C — 712

Spider's Web
  A — 714
  B — 713
  C — 712

Lazy Daisy:
  A — 714
  B — 713
  C — 712
  K — 356

Fly Stitch:
  K — 356

French Knot:
  J — 354

STITCH FORMATION

One strand of Appletons crewel wool has been used for the greenery (fly stitch, lazy daisy and French knots); two strands have been used for the buds, two for the smaller bullions and three for the larger bullions (right front). A single thread is required for the spider's web.

    I found it was a good idea to trail the thread, catching it occasionally in the knit of the garment. This works well if using the same coloured thread within a small area. It is not a good idea to trail your threads if the distance between stitches or groups of stitches is substantial. Items of jewellery, finger-nails and other objects can easily get caught in long, loose threads if they are not firmly secured at the back of the garment.

PROJECTS AND DESIGNS

Right front

43

PROJECTS AND DESIGNS

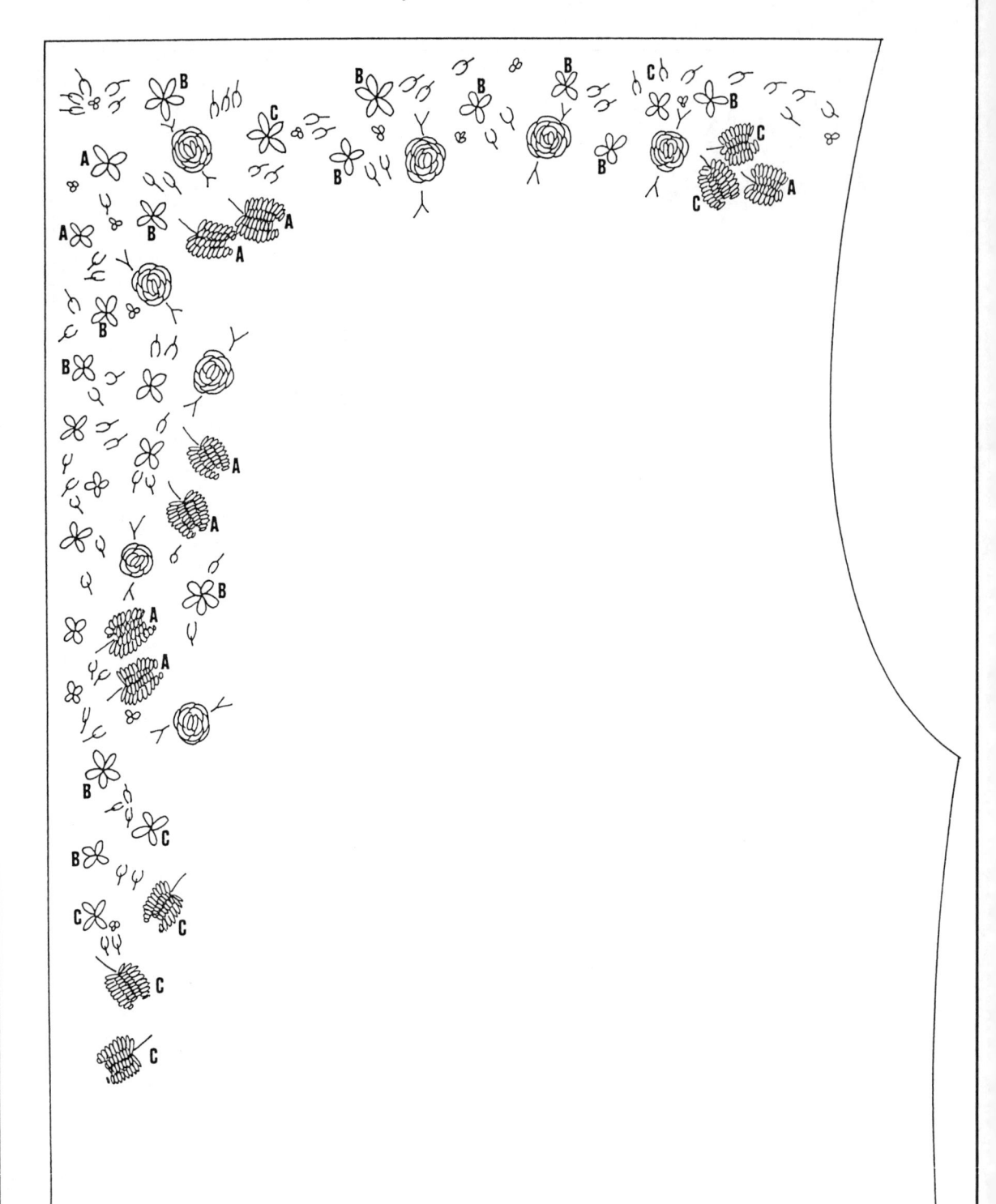

Navy knit cardigan Left front

PROJECTS AND DESIGNS

Centre back

Back

45

Soft-Pink Knit Jumper

A heavier weight of cotton-knit jumper has been used for this project. It has a wide crew neck, the only feature of an otherwise plain garment. The softness of the jumper meant that DMC soft embroidery cottons were most suitable. Soft tones have been used to team with the colour of the garment.

STITCHES

Bullion Rose
Bullion Bud
French Knot
Fly Stitch
Lazy Daisy

COLOURS

All DMC soft embroidery cottons
- B — 2223 Medium dusty pink
- A — 2778 Light dusty pink
- C — 2369 Fern green
- D — Ecru

STITCH COLOURS

Bullion Rose:
- B — 2223 (centres)
- A — 2778 (surround)

Bullion Bud:
- B — 2223

French Knot:
- D — Ecru

Fly Stitch:
- C — 2369

Lazy Daisy:
- C — 2369

STITCH FORMATION

Bullion centres are worked in B — 2223 using all five strands of thread. Surrounding bullions are worked in A — 2778, also using five threads. Bullion buds are stitched in B — 2223, five strands, and two bullions of the same length form the buds.

Lazy daisy petals are worked for the leaves around bullion roses. Use two strands of cotton. Extended fly stitch is used for the greenery around the bullion buds. Use two strands of cotton. Use two strands of cotton in D — Ecru for the French knots.

PROJECTS AND DESIGNS

The stitching on the sleeves features bullion roses and buds, and French knots. The embroidery is worked just above the cuff.

The neck and sleeves have been stitched with a continuous pattern of lazy daisy petals in C — 2369 and French knots, D — Ecru, at the base of the petals along the seam line of neckband and sleeve.

Note: Soft embroidery cotton is unsuitable for use in a single strand, but can be used successfully in multiples.

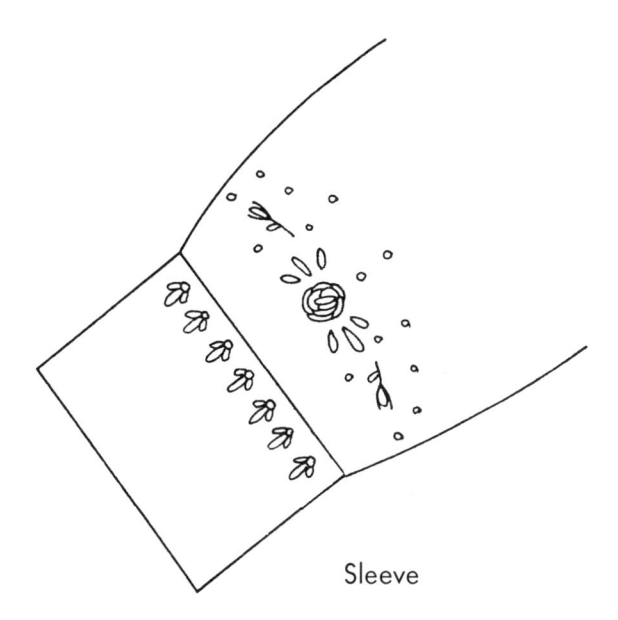

Sleeve

PROJECTS AND DESIGNS

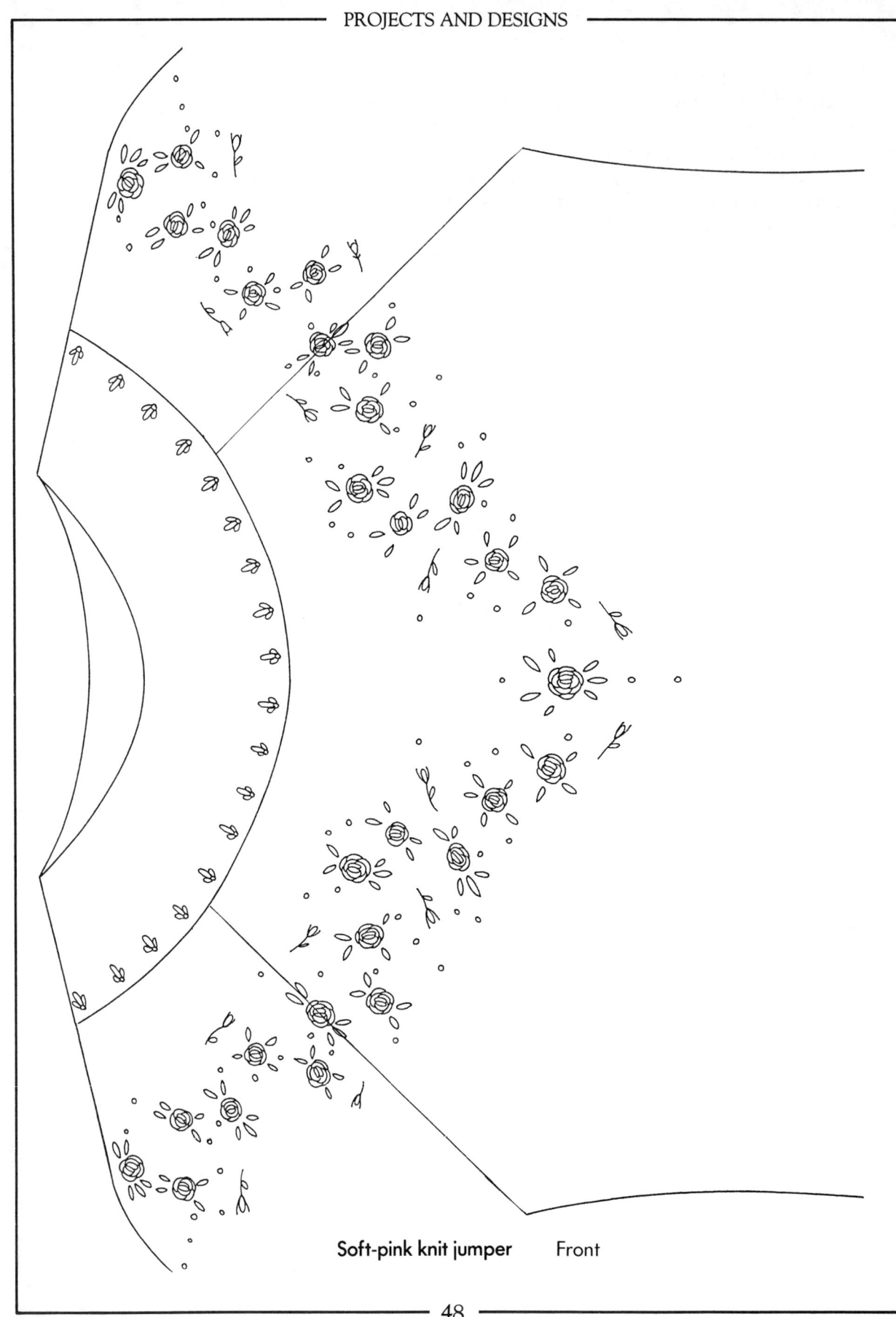

Soft-pink knit jumper   Front

PROJECTS AND DESIGNS

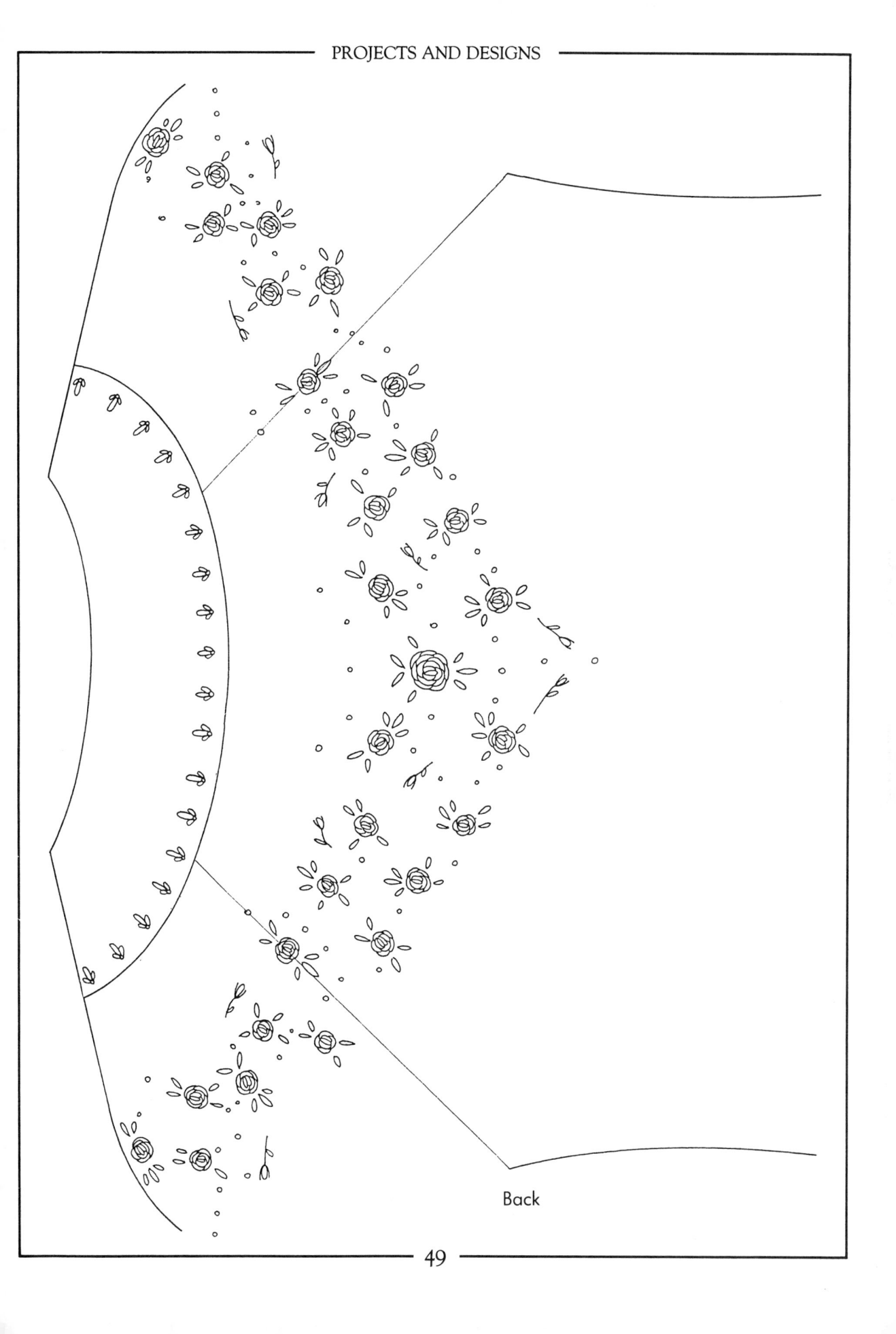

Back

PROJECTS AND DESIGNS

CREAM KNIT JUMPER

This loose-fitting, machine-knitted jumper has drop shoulders, crew neck and deep cuffs, and is hip length. I have worked many colours and only a few stitches into this design, to give character to an otherwise plain garment.

STITCHES

Bullion Rose
Lazy Daisy
Feather Stitch
Fly Stitch

COLOURS

All Appletons crewel wools
    A — 714 Dark dusty pink
    B — 713 Medium dusty pink
    C — 712 Light dusty pink
    D — 711 Lightest dusty pink
    E — 741 Cornflour blue
    F — 601 Pale mauve
    J — 354 Medium green
    R — 222 Medium dusty apricot
    S — 705 Pale apricot

STITCH COLOURS

Bullion Rose:
    A — 714
    B — 713
    C — 712
    E — 741
    F — 601
    R — 222
    S — 705

Lazy Daisy:
    S — 705
    D — 711
    E — 741
    F — 601

Feather Stitch:
    J — 354

Fly Stitch:
    S — 705

STITCH FORMATION

All stitches have been worked with Appletons crewel wools. Bullion roses need two strands, lazy daisies only one. Fly and feather stitches are also worked in one strand.

Note: Cuffs are stitched in a trailing design similar to that of the main body of the jumper. Work the design 3 cm (1 in) from the cuff/sleeve seam. A single thread of wool is used in the following colour sequence: S, D, E, F. Work lazy daisies in these colours. The trailing greenery (J) around large bullions on right shoulder is worked in feather stitch, also using one strand of wool. Lazy daisy petals in J are also stitched around the lazy daisy flowers.

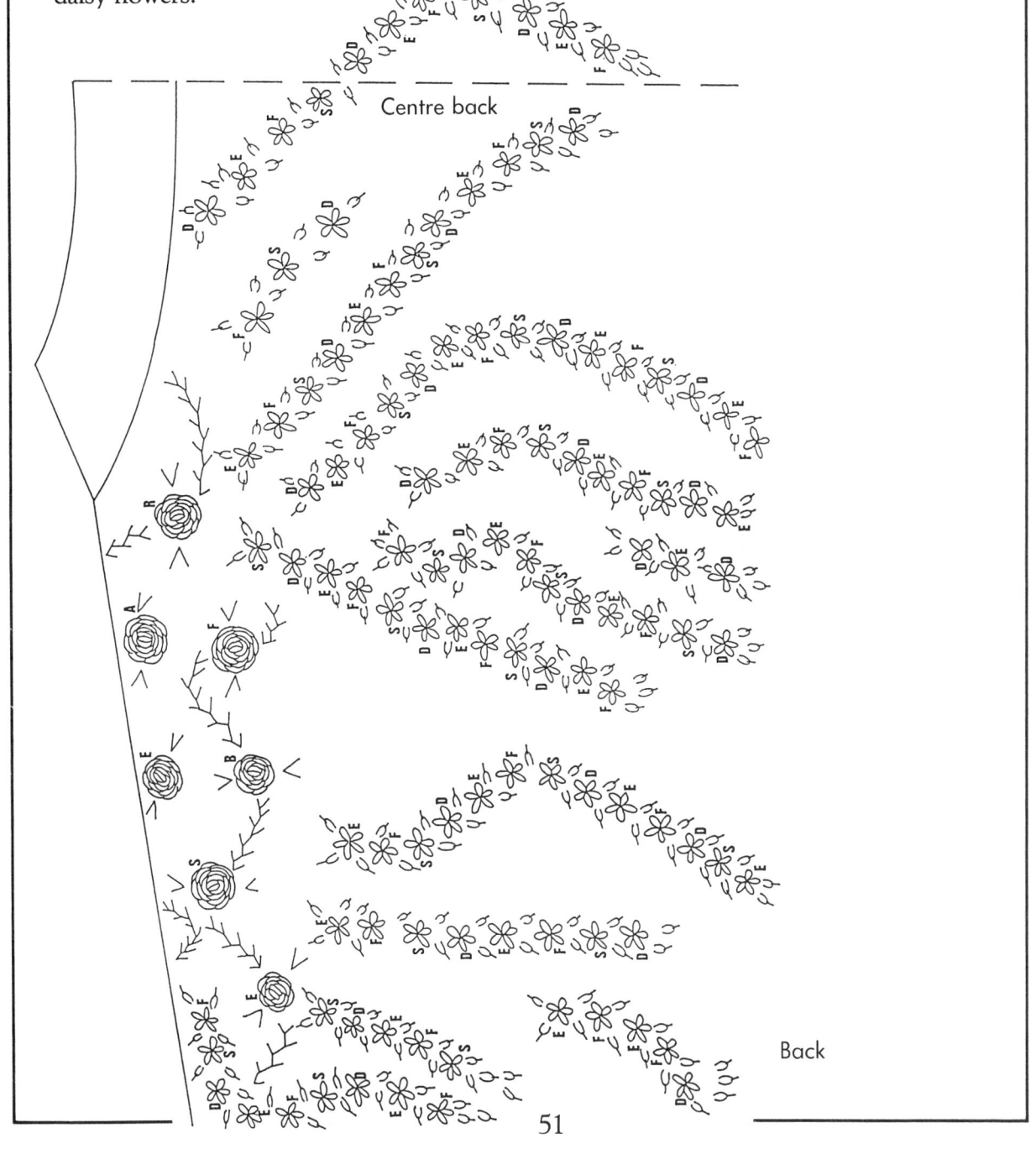

Centre back

Back

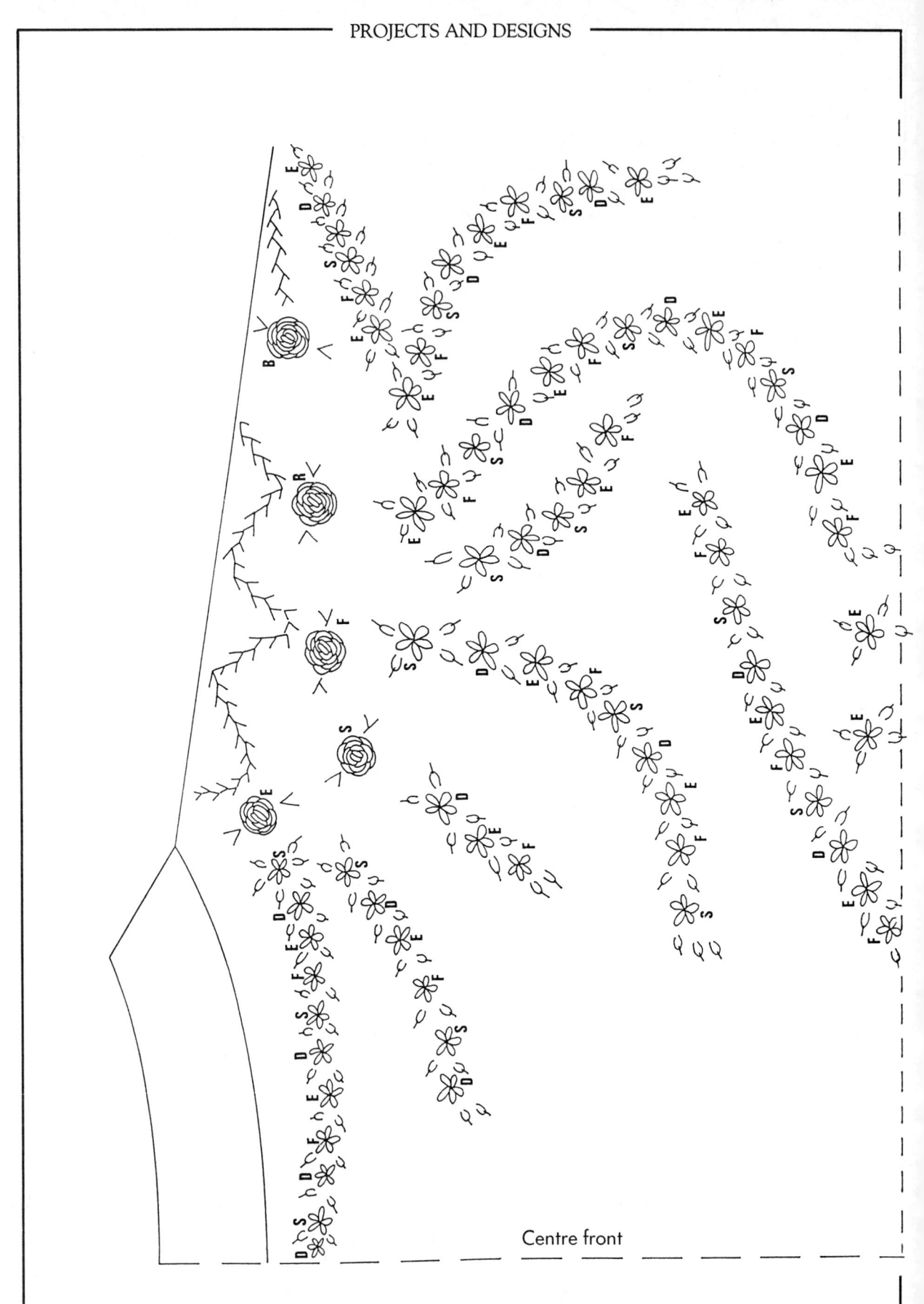

PROJECTS AND DESIGNS

Centre front

PROJECTS AND DESIGNS

Cream knit jumper   Front

NAVY COTTON-KNIT JUMPER

A commercially made, pure cotton jumper in a heavyweight knit has been used for this project. Because the garment has a wide crew neck, a sequence of embroidery was worked between neck band and main body of the garment, and also around the cuffs.

Appletons crewel wools have been used for all the embroidery; the rich, deep red, the grass green and cream are a lovely complement to the navy sweater.

STITCHES

Bullion
Double Fly
French Knot
Lazy Daisy

COLOURS

All Appletons crewel wool
   M — 504 Rich red
   J — 354 Grass green
   P — 881 Cream

STITCH COLOURS

Bullion:
   M — 504

Lazy Daisy:
   M — 504

French Knot:
   P — 881

Double Fly:
   J — 354

STITCH FORMATION

The rich red flowers are worked using a single, central bullion. Beginning directly beneath this, two slightly longer bullions are placed, one to each side as if to encase it. The last bullion is worked around the base of the centre ones, forming a semi-circle that extends from the mid-point of the enclosing bullion on the left-hand side, to the mid point of that on the right-hand side. Use four threads for all bullions.

Double fly stitch is worked with two threads of J — 354 and is used to form foliage around the bullions. The French knot stitched on top of central bullion uses one strand of wool, wrapped twice around the needle.

Double fly stitch is also used in J — 354 around the neck and sleeves, with lazy daisy in M — 504 used

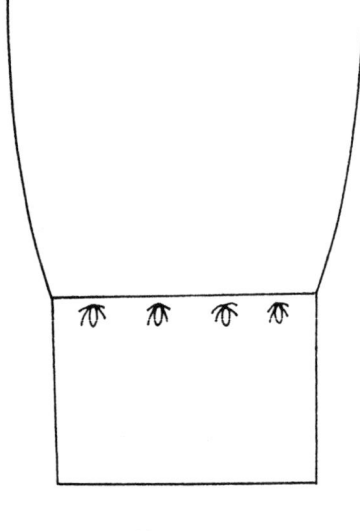

Sleeve

to form the bud. A French knot in P — 881 is stitched into the centre of the lazy daisy. All these stitches are formed with one thread only.

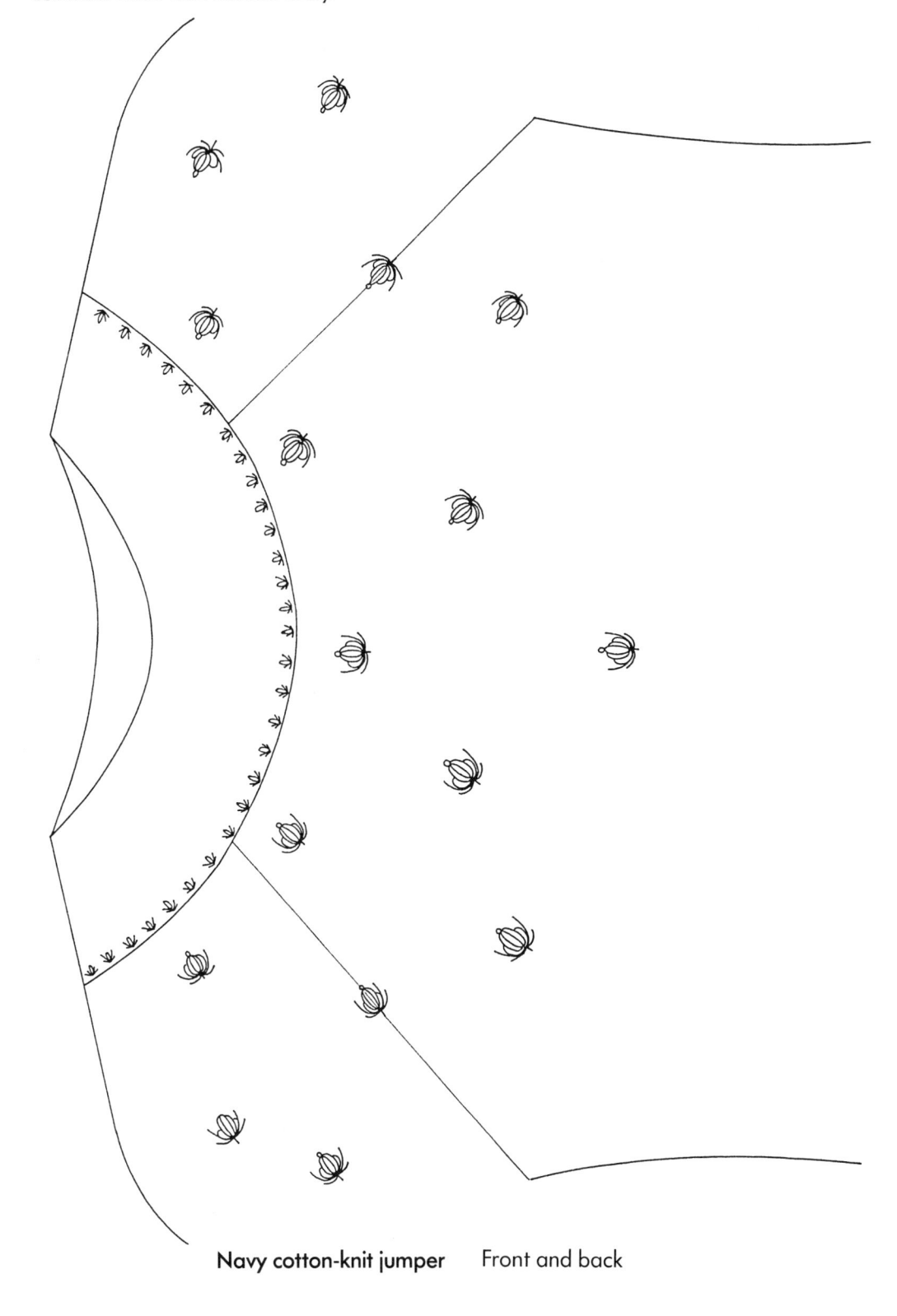

Navy cotton-knit jumper   Front and back

PROJECTS AND DESIGNS

BLACK FINE-KNIT JUMPER

The quality of the jumper is well suited to the design chosen to embellish it. This wool/polyester garment could be hand-washed, but because pure silk ribbon has been worked onto it to form flowers, it is advisable to have it dry cleaned. Dry cleaning is the only successful way to clean items to which silk ribbon has been attached.

STITCHES

Woven Rose
Lazy Daisy
Fly Stitch
French Knot
Feather Stitch

COLOURS

Kanagawa pure silk ribbon
    A — 130 Dark pink
    B — 129 Medium pink
    C — 128 Light pink

DMC stranded cotton
    A — 3731 Dark pink
    F — 501 Green

STITCH COLOURS

Woven Rose:
    Large rose B — 129 (centre) A — 130 (surround)
    Medium rose A — 130 (centre) B — 129 (surround)
    Small rose B — 129 (centre) C — 128 (surround)

Lazy Daisy:
    A — 130

Fly Stitch:
    F — 501

French Knot:
    A — 3731

Feather Stitch:
    F — 501

STITCH FORMATION

All flowers are worked with pure silk ribbon. The green stitches are worked with two strands of DMC stranded cotton, as are the French knots.

Note: Woven rose is formed in the same manner as usual, but by weaving silk ribbon rather than thread over and under the spokes. A French knot is worked into the centre of the roses in the appropriate colour.

PROJECTS AND DESIGNS

Centre front

Front

57

PROJECTS AND DESIGNS

Centre back

Black fine-knit jumper   Back

THREAD GRID

	Stranded cotton	Broder	Soft emb cotton	Pure silk	Appton crewel wool	Silk ribbon	Hand-dyed V crewel
A	3731	818	2778	190	714	130	p035
A2	210						
B	225	776	2223	821	713	129	g036
B2	445						
C	224	white	2369	188	712	128	mp037
C2	800						
D	223	ecru	ecru	7	711	white	
D2	317						
E	221	745	2759	8	741	ecru	
E2	340						
F	501	760	2758	91	601	31	
F2	776						
G	502	761	2357	93	141	32	
G2	840						
H	503	368	2715	140	143	33	
H2	932						
I	504	320	2320	193	351	157	
I2	523						
J	760	952	2393	14	354	158	
K	761	353	2760	174	356	159	
L	819	3325	2329	825	358	87	
M		334	2952	94	504	88	
N	369	3685	2336	141	604	89	
O	368	210	2799	white	701	2	
P	320	336	2745	166	881	4	
Q	367		2209	114	223	15	
R	778		2211	827	222		
S	316		2776	35	705		
T	315		2316	33	754		
U	948		2315	96	755		
V	754		2375		756		
W	353		2522		873		
X	352				877		
Y	318				923		
Z	963				925		

For further information on any of
the products listed contact:
PO Box 975
Shepparton VIC 3630
Australia